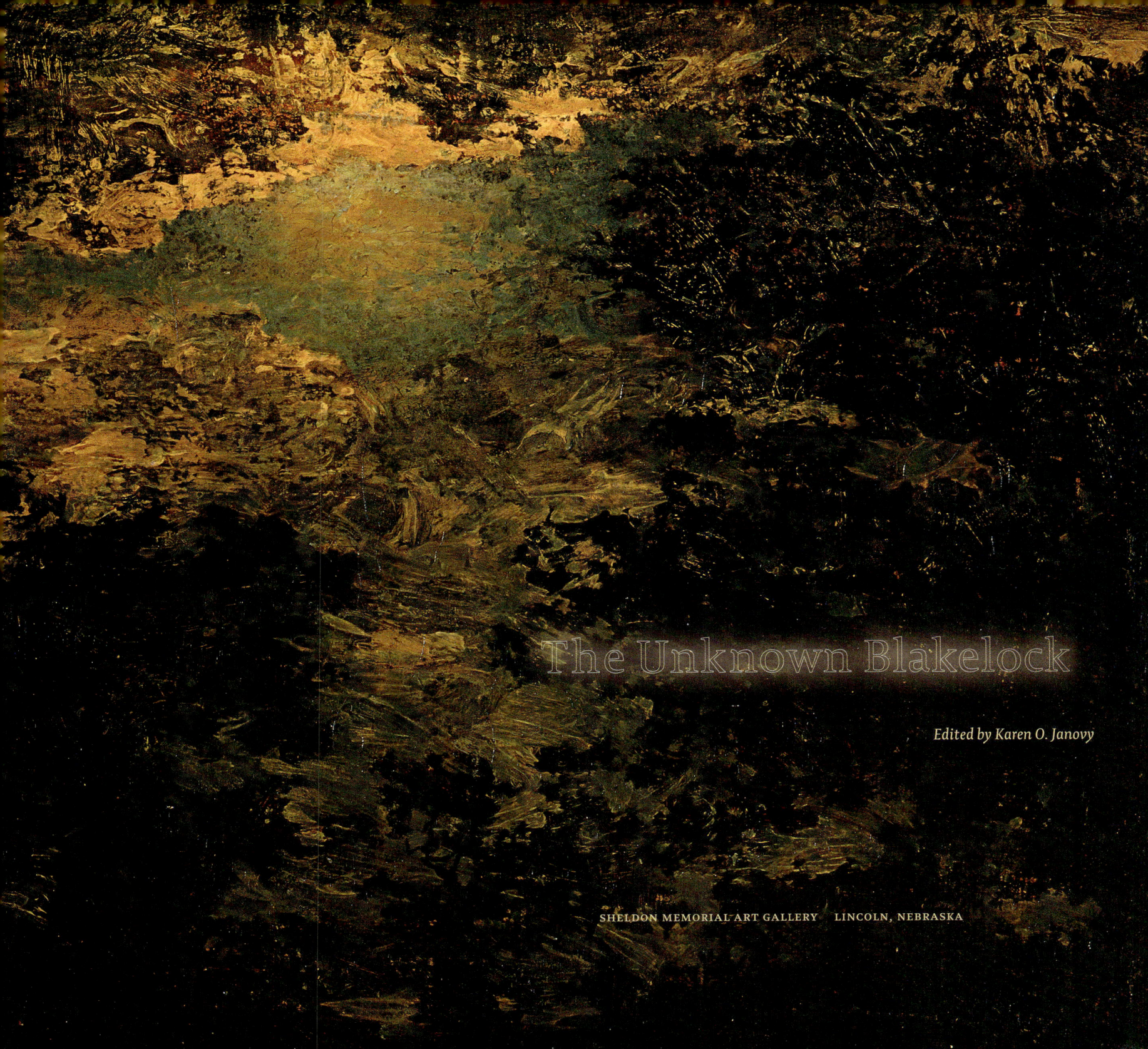

The Unknown Blakelock

Edited by Karen O. Janovy

SHELDON MEMORIAL ART GALLERY   LINCOLN, NEBRASKA

JANUARY 25–AUGUST 24, 2008
Sheldon Memorial Art Gallery
University of Nebraska–Lincoln
Lincoln, Nebraska

SEPTEMBER 25, 2008–JANUARY 4, 2009
National Academy Museum and School of Fine Arts
New York City, New York

This book is published in conjunction with the exhibition *The Unknown Blakelock*.

Funding was provided by the Henry Luce Foundation, the Wyeth Foundation for American Art, Ameritas Charitable Foundation, the Nebraska Arts Council, Ethel S. Abbott Charitable Foundation, and the Nebraska Art Association.

Library of Congress Cataloging-in-Publication Data
     The unknown Blakelock / edited by Karen O. Janovy.
          p. cm.
     Catalog of an exhibition at the Sheldon Memorial Art Gallery, University of Nebraska–Lincoln, Lincoln, NE, Jan.25–Aug. 24, 2008 ; and at the National Academy Museum and School of Fine Arts, New York City, NY., Sept. 25, 2008–Jan. 4, 2009.
     Includes bibliographical references.
     ISBN 978-0-9778028-7-6 (softcover : alk. paper)
     1. Blakelock, Ralph Albert, 1847–1919—Themes, motives—Exhibitions. 2. Blakelock, Ralph Albert, 1847–1919—Criticism and interpretation. I. Janovy, Karen O., 1940–. II. Sheldon Memorial Art Gallery. III. National Academy (U.S.).
ND237.B6A4 2008
759.13—dc22   2008001798

Published by the Sheldon Memorial Art Gallery
P.O. Box 880300
Lincoln, NE 68588-0300
www.sheldonartgallery.org

Distributed by the University of Nebraska Press
www.nebraskapress.unl.edu

Details
Pages 1, 2–3: plate 18, page 64
Page 8: plate 4, page 14
Pages 20–21: plate 9, page 24
Pages 28–29: plate 13, page 38
Pages 52–53: plate 8, page 23

Copyedited by John Pierce
Proofread by Barbara McGill
Designed by Zach Hooker
Typeset by Brynn Warriner
Separations by iocolor, Seattle

Produced by Marquand Books, Inc., Seattle
     www.marquand.com

Printed and bound in China by 1010 Printing International, Ltd.

Contents

List of Plates

The Unknown Blakelock introduces themes other than the characteristic "moonlights" and "Indian encampment" scenes for which Ralph Albert Blakelock is best known. The numbered plates illustrate different aspects of the painter's practice and are grouped accordingly—western landscapes, Native American subjects, Jamaican landscapes, shanty scenes, seascapes, landscapes/skyscapes, still lifes, and imaginary/fantasy compositions.

CHARACTERISTIC MOONLIGHT SCENES

Moonlight, about 1880s, oil on canvas, 22 × 27 in., Sheldon Memorial Art Gallery and Sculpture Garden, University of Nebraska–Lincoln, NAA—Nelle Cochrane Woods Memorial, 1960, N-127 (NBI-304.II), plate 8.

Moonlight, 1886–1895, oil on canvas, 28⅛ × 37⅛ in., The Corcoran Gallery of Art, 26.8, Washington, DC, William A. Clark Collection (NBI-21.I), plate 17.

Heavy Woods—Moonlight, undated, oil on board, 6⅛ × 9¾ in., Sheldon Memorial Art Gallery and Sculpture Garden, University of Nebraska–Lincoln, UNL—Gift of Mrs. Olga N. Sheldon, 1973, U-3286 (NBI-157.I), plate 15.

CHARACTERISTIC INDIAN ENCAMPMENT

Indian Encampment, undated, oil on canvas, 9½ × 13½ in., Gift of Mr. C. R. Smith, 1967.030, Permanent Collection, Snite Museum of Art, University of Notre Dame, Notre Dame, Indiana (NBI-2.II), plate 5.

Representative "Unknown" Blakelocks

WESTERN LANDSCAPE

Rocky Mountains, about 1871, oil on canvas, 33 × 55 in., Berkshire Museum, Pittsfield, Massachusetts (NBI-198.I), plate 6.

THE NATIVE AMERICAN

Going to the Spring, undated, oil on canvas, 8 × 5¾ in., The JPMorgan Chase Art Collection, 36595 (NBI-1030.II), plate 19.

The Snowshoe Dance, 1879, oil on panel, 18 × 30 in., Gilcrease Museum, 0126.1548, Tulsa, Oklahoma (NBI-402.I), plate 20.

JAMAICAN LANDSCAPES

St. Gabriel's Grotto, Isle of Jamaica, about 1872, oil on canvas, 36 × 24 in., The James M. Cowan Collection of American Art, The Parthenon Museum, Nashville, Tennessee (NBI-373.II), plate 2.

The Grotto, 1880, oil on canvas, 36¼ × 56¼ in., Chrysler Museum of Art, Norfolk, Virginia, Gift of Walter P. Chrysler Jr., 71.620, Photograph by Ed Pollard (NBI-507.I), plate 10.

SHANTY SCENES

59th Street in 1864, undated, oil on panel, 7 × 11⅜ in., Des Moines Art Center Permanent Collection, Des Moines, Iowa, Gift of Carl Weeks, 1962.19 (NBI-39.I), plate 3.

Shanties, Seventh Avenue at 55th St., undated, oil on canvas, 16¼ × 24³⁄₁₆ in., Collection of Al and Lisa Schmitt, Los Angeles, California (NBI-463.II), plate 1.

SEASCAPES

Summer, undated, oil on board, 4 × 12 in., Collection of Jane and Carl H. Rohman, Lincoln, Nebraska (NBI-167.I), plate 11.

The Sun, Serene, Sinks into the Slumbrous Sea, undated, oil on canvas, 16 × 24 in., Museum of Fine Arts, Springfield, Massachusetts, Horace P. Wright Collection (NBI-224.I), plate 4.

LANDSCAPE/SKYSCAPE

After Sundown, before 1897, oil on canvas, 27⅛ × 37¼ in., © Addison Gallery of American Art, Phillips Academy, Andover, Massachusetts (NBI-291.I), plate 13.

STILL LIFES

Japanese Lantern and Moths, undated, oil on board, 8 × 4⅝ in., Collection of Mr. and Mrs. Walter Blakelock Wilson, Tubac, Arizona (NBI-1851.I), plate 21.

Carnations and Zinnias, about 1875–77, oil on panel, 11½ × 7¼ in., Collection of Teresa Heinz (NBI-241.I), plate 12.

FANTASY, IMAGINATION, AND EXPRESSIONISM

Woodland Brook, 1880s–1890s, oil on canvas, 16 × 24 in., Collection Albright-Knox Art Gallery, 1977.6, Buffalo, New York, Gift of Elizabeth Elser Doolittle Charitable Trust, 1977 (NBI-434. I), plate 16.

Moonlight, Silver and Old Lace, about 1880s, oil on canvas, 16⅛ × 24⅛ in., Santa Barbara Museum of Art, 1947.22.1, Santa Barbara, California, Gift of Mr. and Mrs. John D. Graham (NBI-95. II), plate 18.

Pegasus, before 1913, oil on canvas, 9 × 13 in., Denver Art Museum, Denver, Colorado, The Edward and Tullah Hanley Memorial, Gift to the People of Denver and the Area, 1974.420 (NBI-68.I), plate 7.

At Nature's Mirror, about 1880, oil on canvas, 16⅛ × 24 in., Smithsonian American Art Museum, Washington, DC, Gift of William T. Evans, 109.7.5 (NBI-242.I), plate 14.

Maiden in the Mist, undated, oil on board, 7⅛ × 21⅞ in., The Grey Collection, Brookville, New York (NBI-2021.II), plate 9.

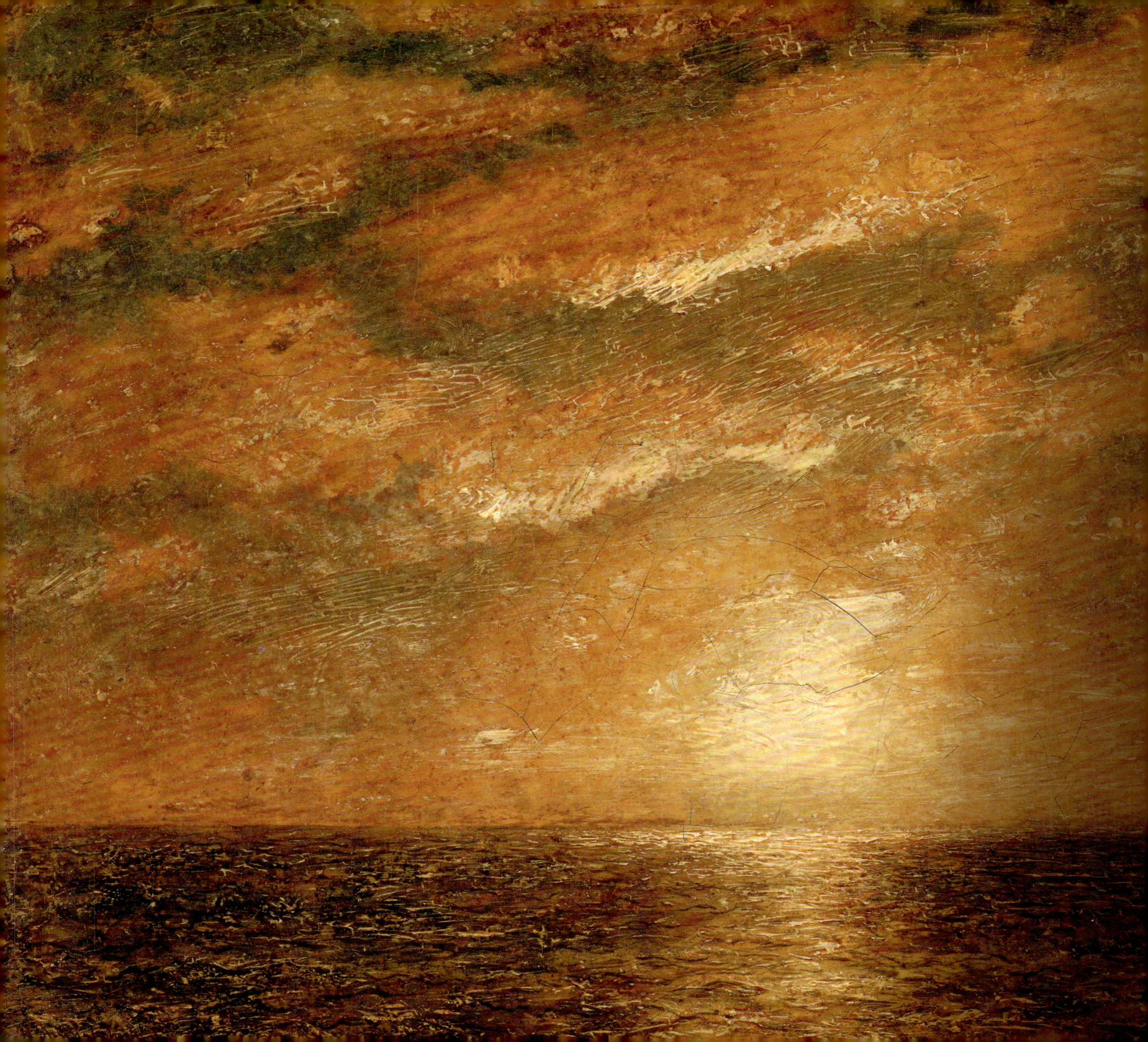

Foreword and Acknowledgments

JANICE DRIESBACH

The Sheldon Memorial Art Gallery has led the examination of the artistic contributions made by Ralph Albert Blakelock (1847–1919) since long before the museum opened its doors in 1963. In the late 1920s, *Evening Glow*, attributed to Blakelock, entered the University of Nebraska collections as part of its first major gift—the bequest from F. M. Hall, an early Lincoln arts benefactor. Hall's acquisitions endowment later funded the purchase of sixty-six works on paper and a painting by Blakelock. In the 1960s, the museum's acquisition of our impressive *Moonlight* (plate 8), a large composition by Blakelock's standards and a signature subject, enriched our representation of late nineteenth-century romantic artists. The Sheldon now has works by a number of figures associated with Blakelock, including George Fuller, Eugene Higgins, George Inness, Robert Loftin Newman, and Albert Pinkham Ryder.

Following the purchase of *Moonlight*, F. duPont Cornelius, at that time the conservator at the Colorado Springs Fine Arts Center, alerted Norman Geske, then the Sheldon's director, to a group of works owned by Blakelock's descendants. As a result, eleven paintings and seven drawings in the collection of Mrs. Ralph M. Blakelock were acquired by the Nebraska Art Association, the Sheldon's dedicated support group. That acquisition expanded the museum's representation of Blakelock's subjects to include such diverse motifs as a scene from Acapulco, *Children in a Hen House*, and unusual landscape views of a striking sunset and a snow-covered scene.

Subsequent projects, including four seminars organized by Geske, brought together hundreds of paintings and drawings associated with this challenging (and much copied) artist. By comparing attributed and purported Blakelocks with undisputed paintings with secure provenance, Geske became a distinguished authority on the artist. These seminars—held in Santa Barbara, California; Lincoln, Nebraska; and twice at the Heckscher Museum on Long Island—were critical to Geske in establishing the Nebraska Blakelock Inventory, which is held at Love Library at the University of Nebraska–Lincoln. The inventory, which continues to grow as new compositions are brought to Geske's attention, now numbers over two thousand examples. The works have been judged from authentic to "clearly not by the artist," and some are in compromised condition that does not permit scholarly evaluation.

Our exhibition *The Unknown Blakelock* was stimulated in part by the publication of Geske's long-awaited critical review of Blakelock's life and work, *Beyond Madness: The Art of Ralph Blakelock, 1847–1919*, from the University of Nebraska Press. In addition to focusing attention on an underappreciated artist, the exhibition seeks to redress the impression that Blakelock's repertoire of subjects was limited to the moonlight and Indian encampment scenes that first earned him a significant reputation. The popularity of these subjects, and the high prices they realized early in the twentieth century, encouraged the indigent artist to return to these established motifs—sometimes in hastily rendered versions—and resulted in scores of optimistic attributions and outright forgeries.

But as Glyn Vincent has demonstrated in his biography of Blakelock[1]—and paintings in private and public collections scattered throughout the United States amply illustrate—Blakelock turned his attention and imagination, which were not limited by academic training, to a range of subjects. Artists associated with an iconic motif or signature style are not often appreciated for their forays into other areas. Our understanding of Blakelock's career—challenged by the difficulty to securely date most of his compositions—seems to have particularly suffered in this regard.

Although he was essentially self-taught and conducted much of his career outside traditional art venues, Blakelock exhibited in and attended receptions for exhibitions at the National Academy of Design, and several times he had studio space alongside major luminaries of his day. While many of his compositions are "singularly free of any allegiance to established procedures,"[2] Blakelock surely was familiar with his milieu and the work of his contemporaries, as well as its reception in the critical press of the day. And although he is traditionally associated with modest-size compositions, some surely by-products of his poverty and his resulting need to sell paintings for small sums, *Indian Encampment* (plate 5, Snite Museum collection) reveals that Blakelock could undertake an ambitious canvas that would "conform with the accepted standards of the day and the expectations of public exhibition." This work is an example of the artist's engagement with western landscape themes in the early 1870s, at a time when his somewhat older contemporaries Albert Bierstadt and Thomas Moran were earning fame for their scenes of Yosemite Valley and Yellowstone, respectively. *Indian Encampment along the Snake River* (in the Anschutz Collection in Denver) is distinguished for its "spatial largeness and depth, variety of details, and . . . polished handling" and aligns Blakelock with the conventions of his time.

As Ralph Albert Blakelock painted landscapes inspired by the western travels he undertook on his own between 1869 and 1873, so he depicted Indian figures, both as colorful details and independent themes. As Vincent notes, Blakelock was not

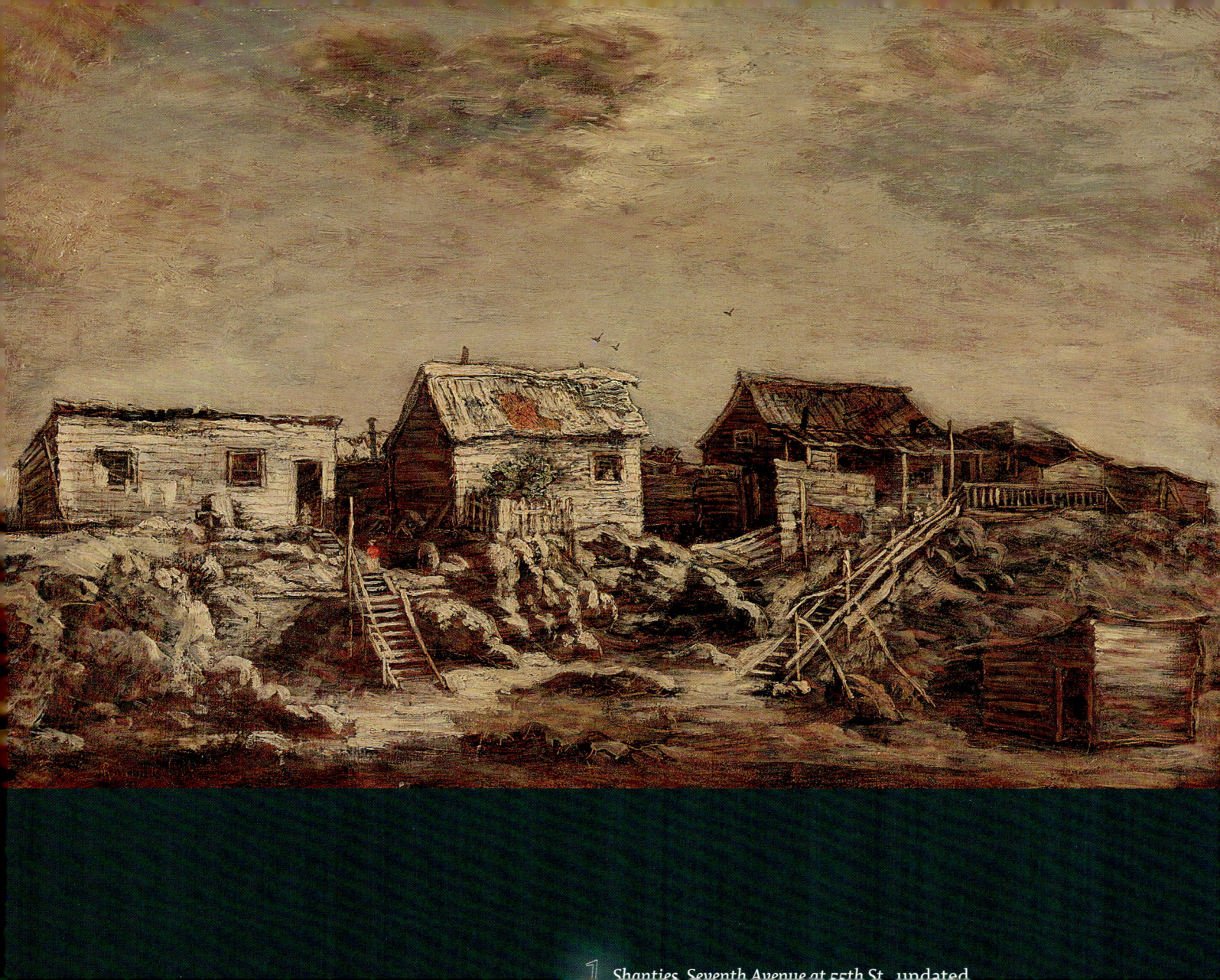

Shanties, Seventh Avenue at 55th St., undated

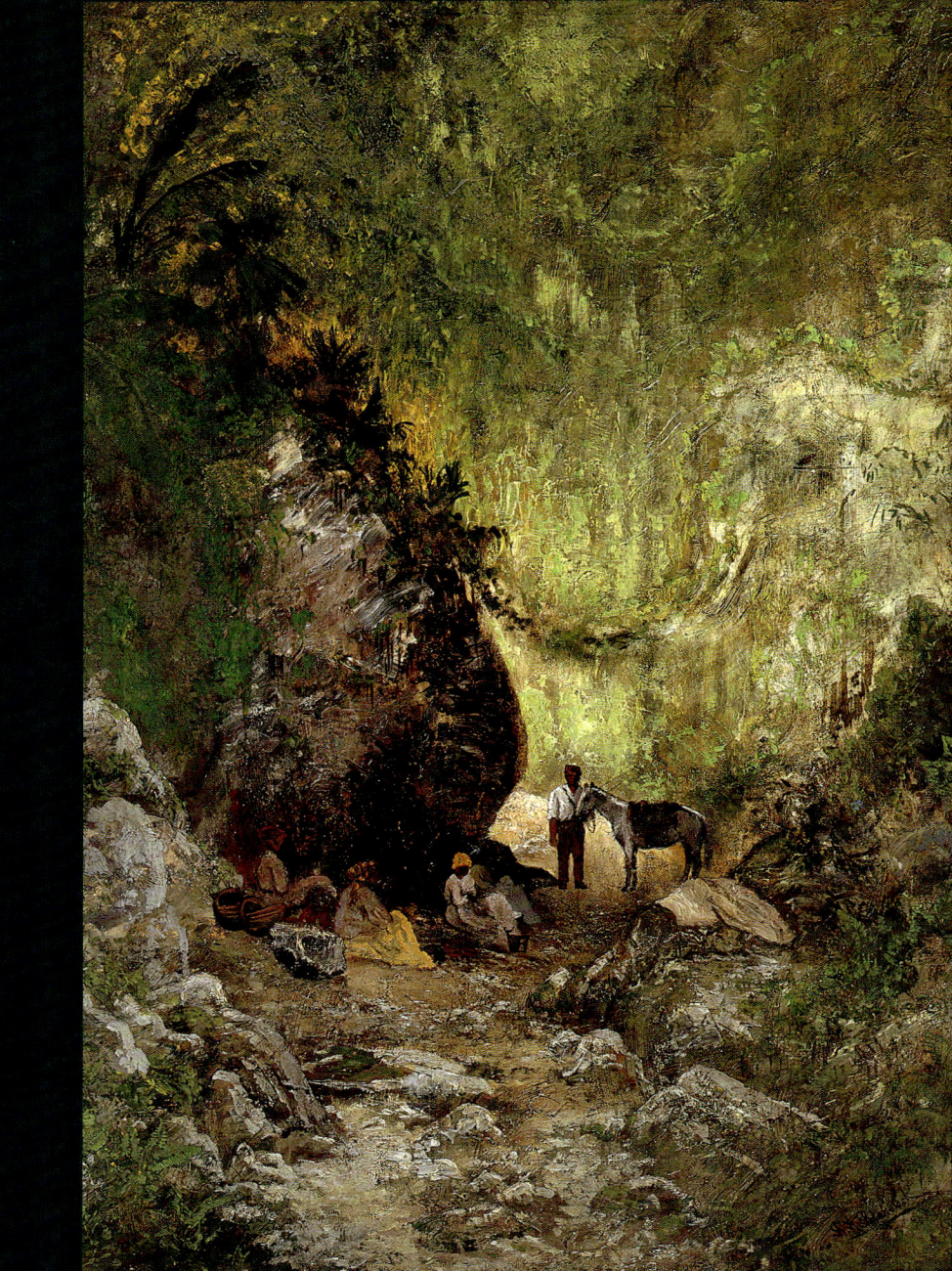

St. Gabriel's Grotto, Isle of Jamaica, about 1872

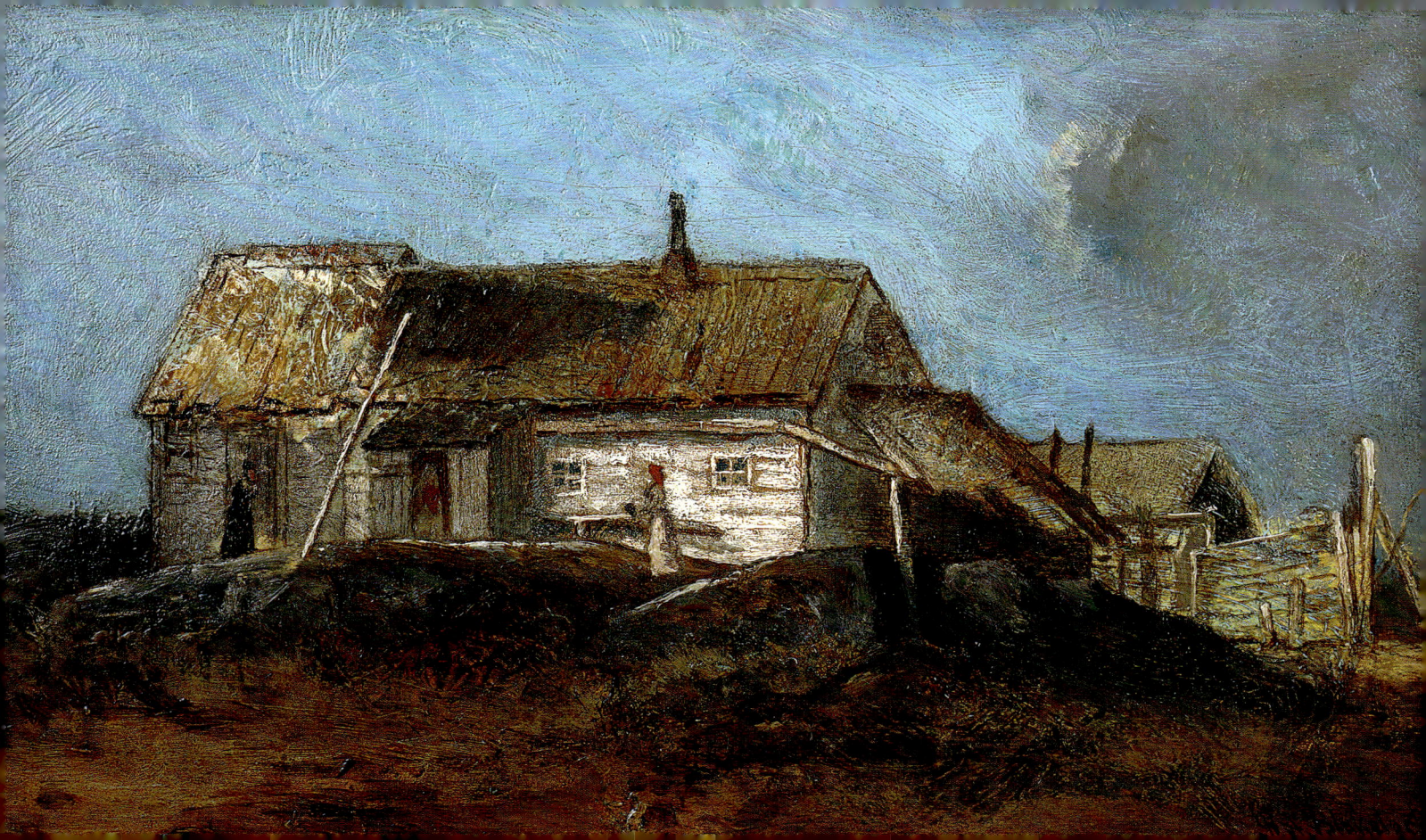

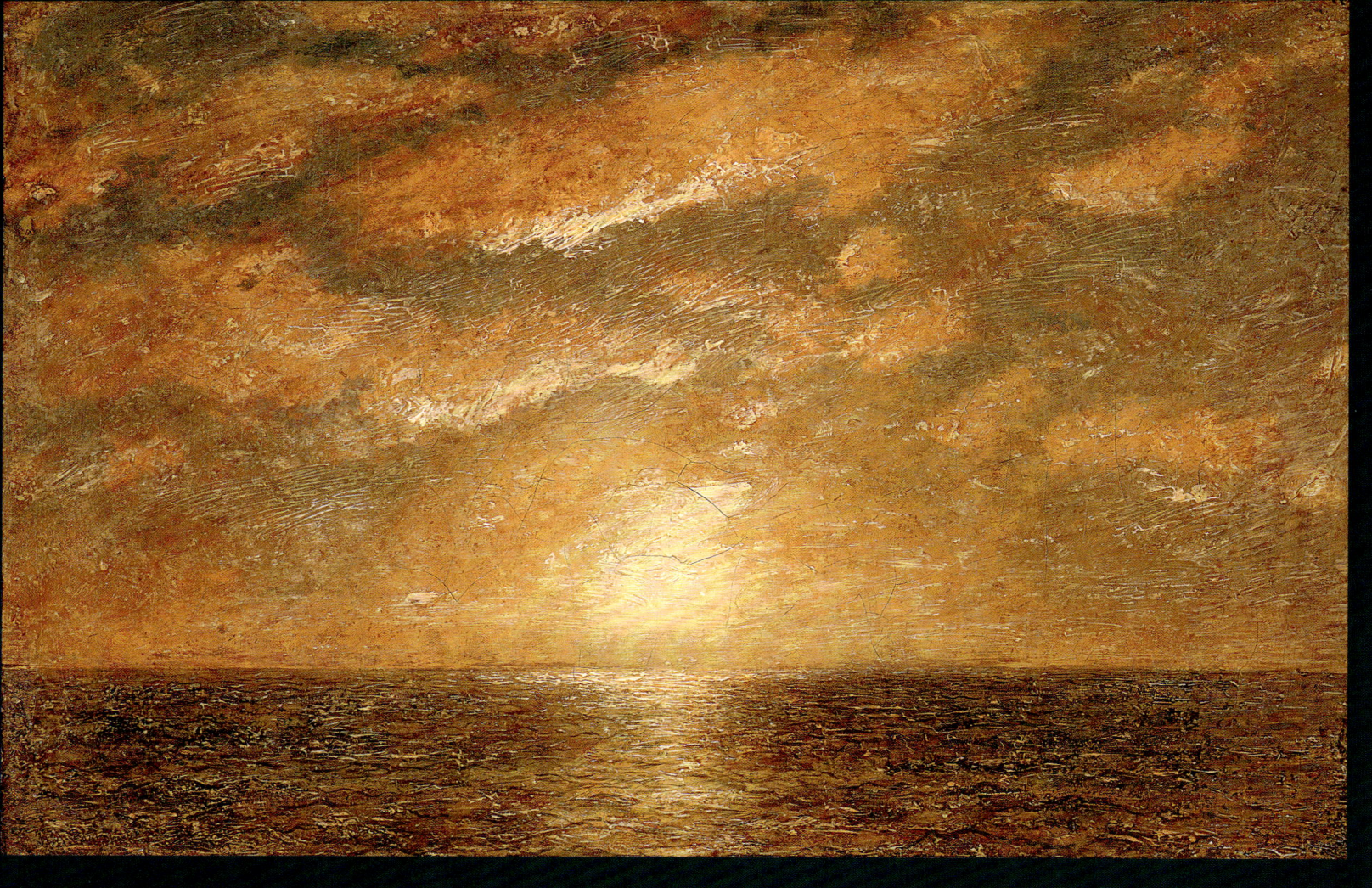

4 *The Sun, Serene, Sinks into the Slumbrous Sea,* undated

interested in depicting anthropological details, but "[w]hen Blakelock does portray Indians, . . . it is in a humane and sympathetic light."[3]

Although many of Blakelock's western views portray scenes the artist encountered on his journeys (in contrast to the artist's later imaginative views), most were likely composed in New York from sketches made on the spot, and many may date from a later time. In contrast, Blakelock's three scenes of Jamaica, where he stopped on his return from his first trip west, were likely created as immediate responses to an extraordinary subject. *St. Gabriel's Grotto* (plate 2) is typical of these paintings in its departure from Blakelock's earlier work, especially in the dominance given to, in Geske's words, "a painterly handling of foliage and the rock formation." Geske continues that "human figures are present, but they are subordinated to the luxuriant backdrop of nondescriptive color," and he notes that "[t]hese paintings display the sensuous lure of the medium that is at the core of Blakelock's creative impulse."

As Blakelock's interest was piqued by subjects he encountered on distant travels, he responded to unconventional motifs closer to home. Among these were the shanties that squatters constructed in what were then unsettled areas of Manhattan. *59th Street in 1864* (plate 3) is an example of these compositions, which depart as well from the "inventive views of encampments and the moonlights" associated with the artist. Notably, these works offer realistic observations of "a rough and undeveloped terrain and buildings of an improvised character in random arrangements."

Although landscape was Blakelock's predominant concern, the sea captured his attention at least twice, inspiring unusual canvases. Land and sky are severely divided into two fields in *The Sun, Serene, Sinks into the Slumbrous Sea* (plate 4), a painting that is "a celebration of color; a curtain, above and below, of flickering reds and yellows."

And although many of the artist's nocturnes were inspired as much by imagination as by external stimuli, Blakelock also created a number of compositions that might best be described as imaginary or fantasy scenes. Paintings such as *Pegasus* (plate 7), may function as landscapes, but they also communicate in "the language of painting, pure and simple. Pigment is allowed to form its own structures, pigment on a flat surface, a construct of unprecedented character in its own time."

The Unknown Blakelock offers opportunities for new visual insights, and observations by Geske, whose study of the artist has spanned decades, are accompanied by essays from Sheldon curator Daniel A. Siedell and Mark D. Mitchell, curator of American art at the Philadelphia Museum of Art, that offer perspectives of a younger generation of scholars. Blakelock's appeal to contemporary audiences, including practicing artists, was confirmed by Dr. Annette Blaugrund, director of the National Academy Museum and School of Fine Arts. Blakelock's work in the museum's collection, acquired because he was an Academician, is among the favorites of current artist members. Dr. Blaugrund has been instrumental in promoting *The Unknown Blakelock* and its presentation in New York.

The Academy would like to thank its former curator Mark Mitchell for his work on this catalogue and its senior curator of nineteenth-century art, Dr. Bruce Weber, who is supervising the exhibition at the Academy. The National Academy appreciates the generous support of its Durand Society; the lead contribution by Questroyal Fine Art, LLC; and the support of its other funders.

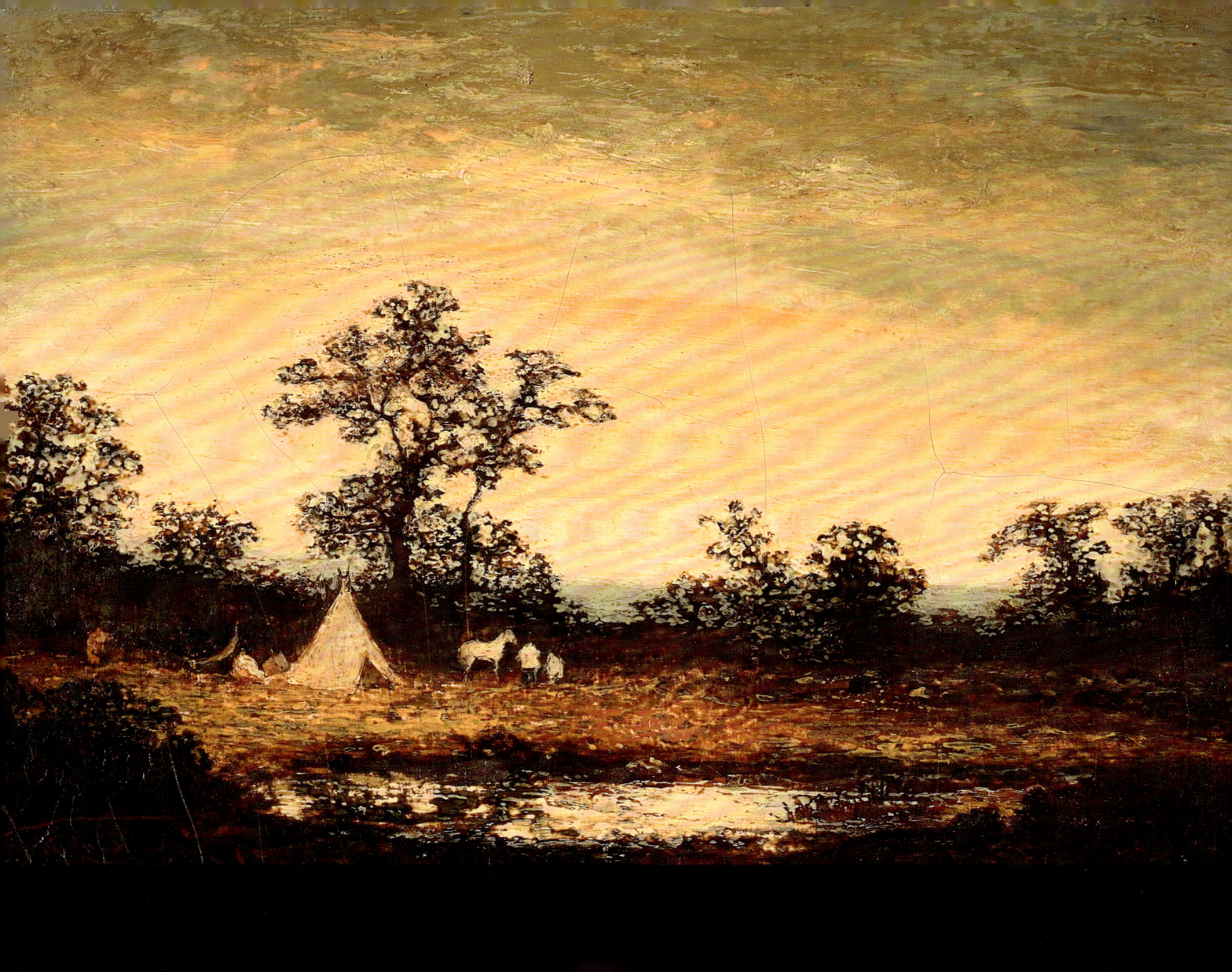

5 *Indian Encampment*, undated

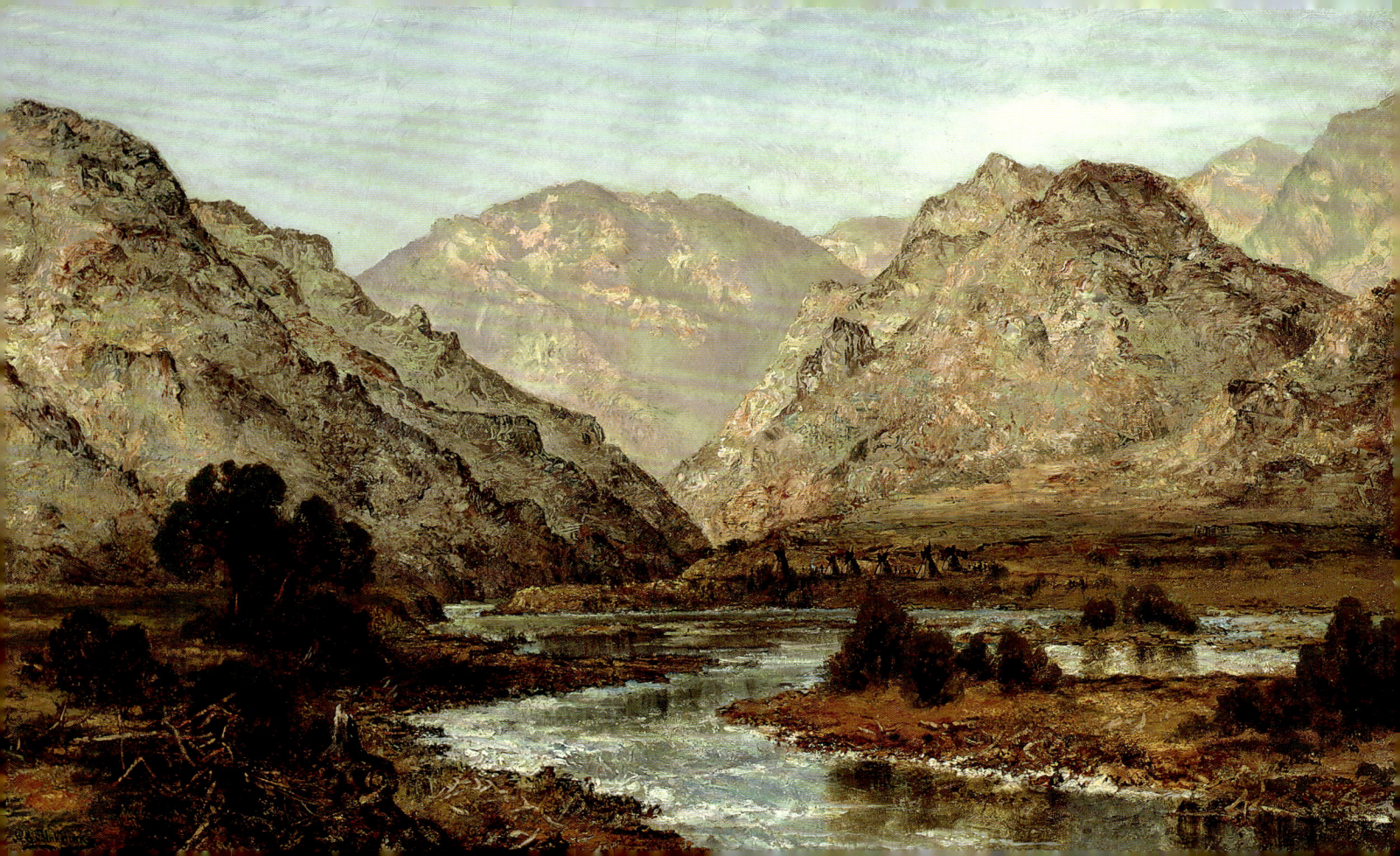

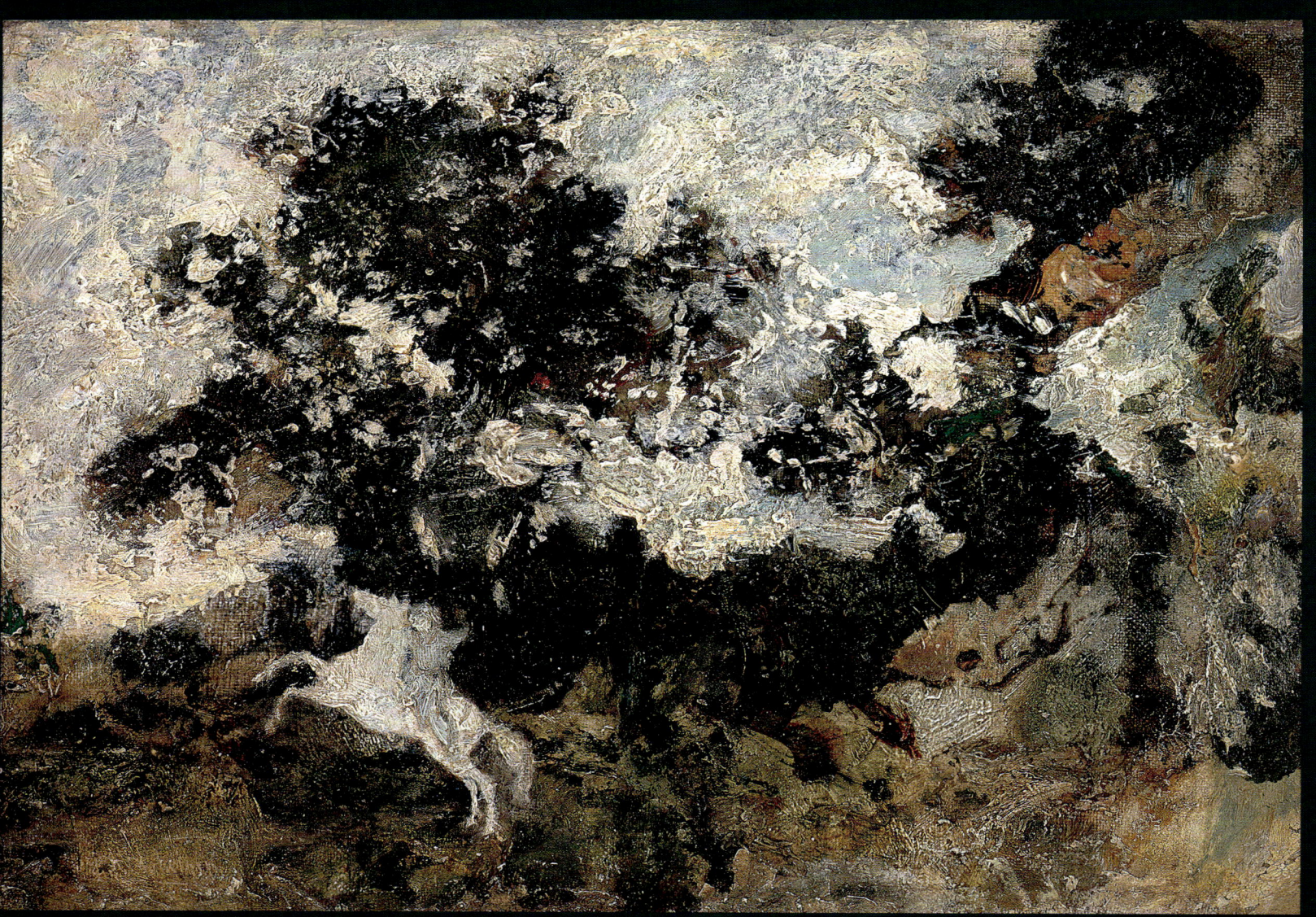

We are deeply grateful to the Henry Luce Foundation for their generous support, which was essential to the development of *The Unknown Blakelock* exhibition, publication, and accompanying programs. Additional funding is provided by the Wyeth Foundation for American Art, Ameritas Charitable Foundation, the Nebraska Arts Council, Ethel S. Abbott Charitable Foundation, and the Nebraska Art Association. The participation of generous museum and private lenders has truly made this ambitious exhibition possible.

Norman Geske and Daniel A. Siedell identified the key works that comprise the exhibition, and Sheldon interim curator Sharon L. Kennedy has guided the project to fruition. Sheldon Memorial Art Gallery collection managers Stacey Walsh and (formerly) Shannan Kelly provided invaluable assistance in overseeing loan requests and making insurance and shipping arrangements, assisted by Gary Rattigan. Project coordinator Laurie Sipple capably secured the images and reproduction rights for the current publication. Exhibition technicians Edson Rumbaugh and Neil Christensen oversaw the installation of the exhibition at the Sheldon, and education curator Karen Janovy oversaw production of the catalogue; designed engaging programs, including a related interpretive display; and trained the museum's talented and enthusiastic docent groups. Interim director Richard J. Hoffmann, administrator Monica Babcock, marketing manager Thomas White, security and facilities manager Lynn Doser, accounting technician Jacqueline Toman, Hixson-Lied/Sheldon Fellow Sarah Barnard Blitz, project assistant Abbey Siebler, and museum store manager Vonni Sparks have likewise been instrumental to the success of the exhibition.

Sheldon Memorial Art Gallery director 2000–2007, Janice Driesbach is now director of The Dayton Art Institute, Dayton, Ohio.

NOTES

1. Glyn Vincent, *The Unknown Night: The Genius and Madness of R. A. Blakelock, An American Painter* (New York: Grove Press, 2003).

2. This and subsequent quotations that are not otherwise attributed are comments Norman Geske has shared in numerous meetings in the course of developing *The Unknown Blakelock* exhibition.

3. Vincent, 103.

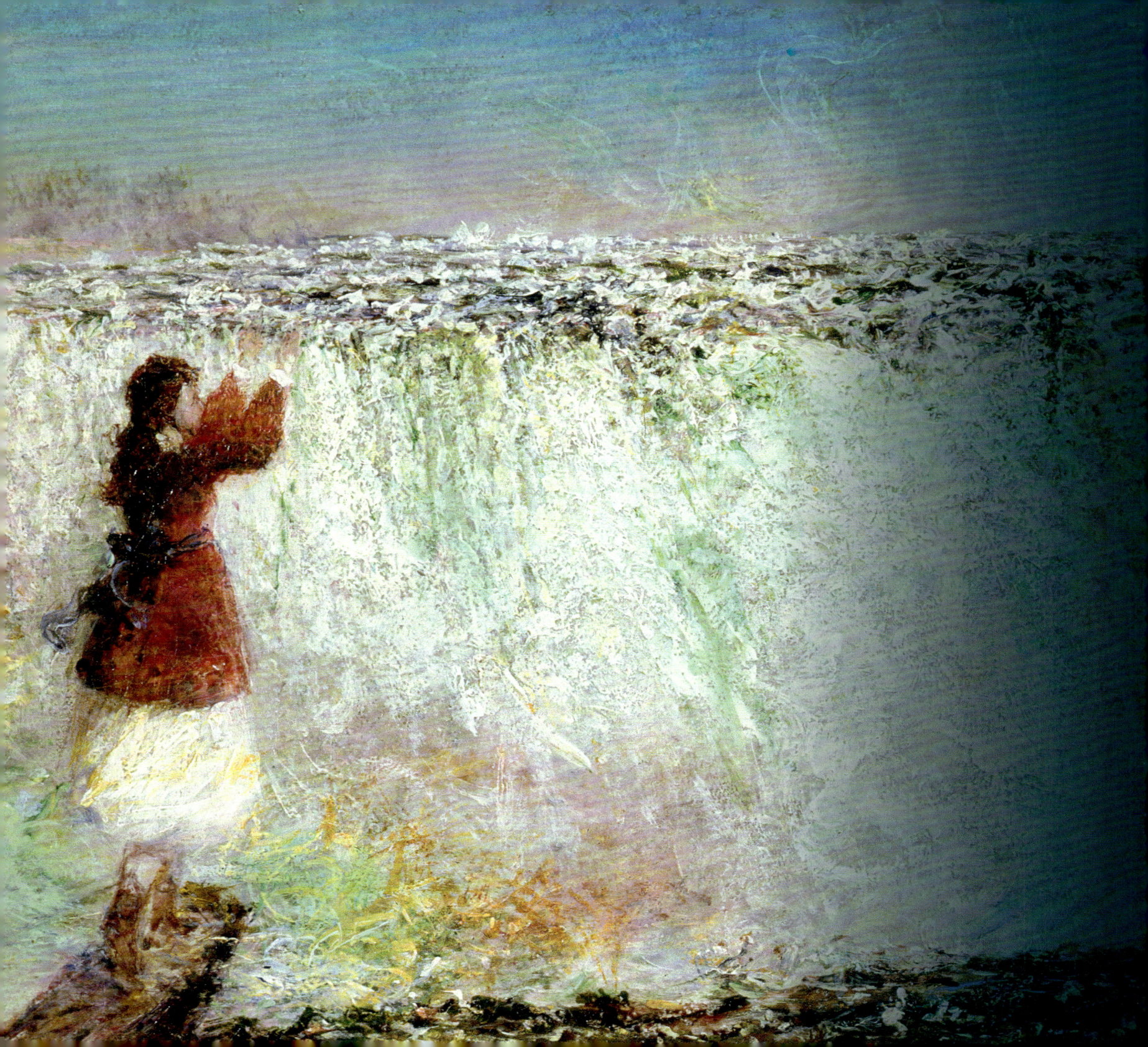

Identifying the Unknown Blakelock

NORMAN A. GESKE

The Sheldon Memorial Art Gallery acquired R. A. Blakelock's *Moonlight* in 1960 (plate 8). The work was seen as an example of the artist's best-known subject matter, but it was an example with a difference. Although *Moonlight* contains all the requisite themes—a nocturnal sky, a dark landscape, moonlight reflected in water—the image is reduced to near abstraction, a wholly subjective transformation of experience. The subject is subsumed within the medium; oil paint is made to speak for itself.

To digress for a moment, this painting is a striking demonstration of one of Blakelock's most idiosyncratic practices. It is notable that as a preliminary for a considerable number of his works, he would lay down on the canvas or panel an undercoat of a freely brushed substance resembling plaster, French chalk, or talc, with no intention of creating a correspondence with the image that he would lay over it. This surface was then rubbed dry to eliminate peaks and ridges. The artist's daughter Ruth recalled seeing her father holding such a panel under the tap to blur the pattern and afterward rubbing it down again with pumice to produce a smooth yet textured surface. The Sheldon's *Moonlight* shows the result: the ephemera of moonlight, reality transformed.

The ability to step outside habit; to cross the line of established convention; to discover a new awareness of space, color, and form is at the heart of *The Unknown Blakelock*. If one reviews the span of the artist's activity, it is immediately apparent that a chronological development of style—his manner of working—is difficult, if not impossible, to describe. At the beginning, little more can be seen than the work of a novice copying his mentor. Later, his brief period of education at New York's Free

Academy amounted to some small acquaintance with anatomy. Essentially from the beginning, he was on his own in the learning process, free to exercise his innate perceptions of how the world looked.

Blakelock paid his respects to the dominating fashion of the Hudson River School in a major effort that, it must be admitted, proved that he could do it but was an accomplishment that did not take. Of Barbizon, there is ample evidence that he was aware of the innovations in the work of the French painters. Their view of nature was, like his own, subjective and inventive.

The optical realism of full-blown impressionism was not part of his vision, but impressionism had his attention in some high-keyed beach scenes that reflect the quasi-impressionism of Johan Jongkind or Eugene Boudin. There is also one moment that seems to indicate that he saw some of Claude Monet's Rouen Cathedral series at Durand-Ruel's New York gallery: three little paintings—painterly, rich, and sensuous—that depict the same subject in the morning, at noon, and at night. With no commitment to academic method or to the fashion of the moment, he approached each work with a fresh eye, loyal only to his own perceptions.

In his travels in the West, in Jamaica, or closer to home in the upper reaches of Manhattan, he found something new—not only different subject matter, but new ways of seeing—in the blazing of light in the western landscape, the enveloping luxuriance of the tropics, and the picturesque realism of people, buildings, and weather. In each of these modes, there seems to be another artist at work, completely at home in these different ways of seeing.

These digressions demonstrate the spontaneous flow of the artist's creativity in images that are very different from the "moonlights" and "Indian encampments" for which he is best known. It is worth noting that in each instance there is nothing like them in the painting of the time. The characteristic that links these works more than any other is the evidence of Blakelock's love of the painter's medium. It is transparent and dry in the western subjects, sensuous and atmospheric in the tropics, and briskly realistic in the depiction of the terrain, buildings, figures, and weather in the shanty paintings. This capacity for inventing new solutions in the face of new experiences sets him apart from his closest contemporaries—Albert Pinkham Ryder, George Fuller, and Robert Loftin Newman—whose work is more or less consistent from beginning to end. In a sense Blakelock was self-taught throughout his career and was always independent of expectations.

A recent, purely fortuitous development in the continuous flow of works attributed to the artist that have come to the attention of the Nebraska Blakelock Inventory is an extraordinary painting that epitomizes in every way the very idea of the unknown Blakelock. In an unusual format, seven by twenty-one inches, it depicts Niagara Falls in a view that illustrates the traditional legend of "The Maid of the Mist." The use of an exact location is rare in itself, but even more unusual is his design for the subject. We are at the very brink of the falls, the depth of the gorge invisible. The foreground is filled with foaming water. The opposite edge is white with spray, and against it there is the hint of a rainbow. At the left, poised at the edge, is the figure of a woman, arms raised, the sacrificial figure of the legend. Above, along the entire upper length of the scene, is an opalescent sky and a barely suggested wooded horizon.

At first it seems hardly possible that this painting can be the work of Blakelock. Aside from the unusual composition,

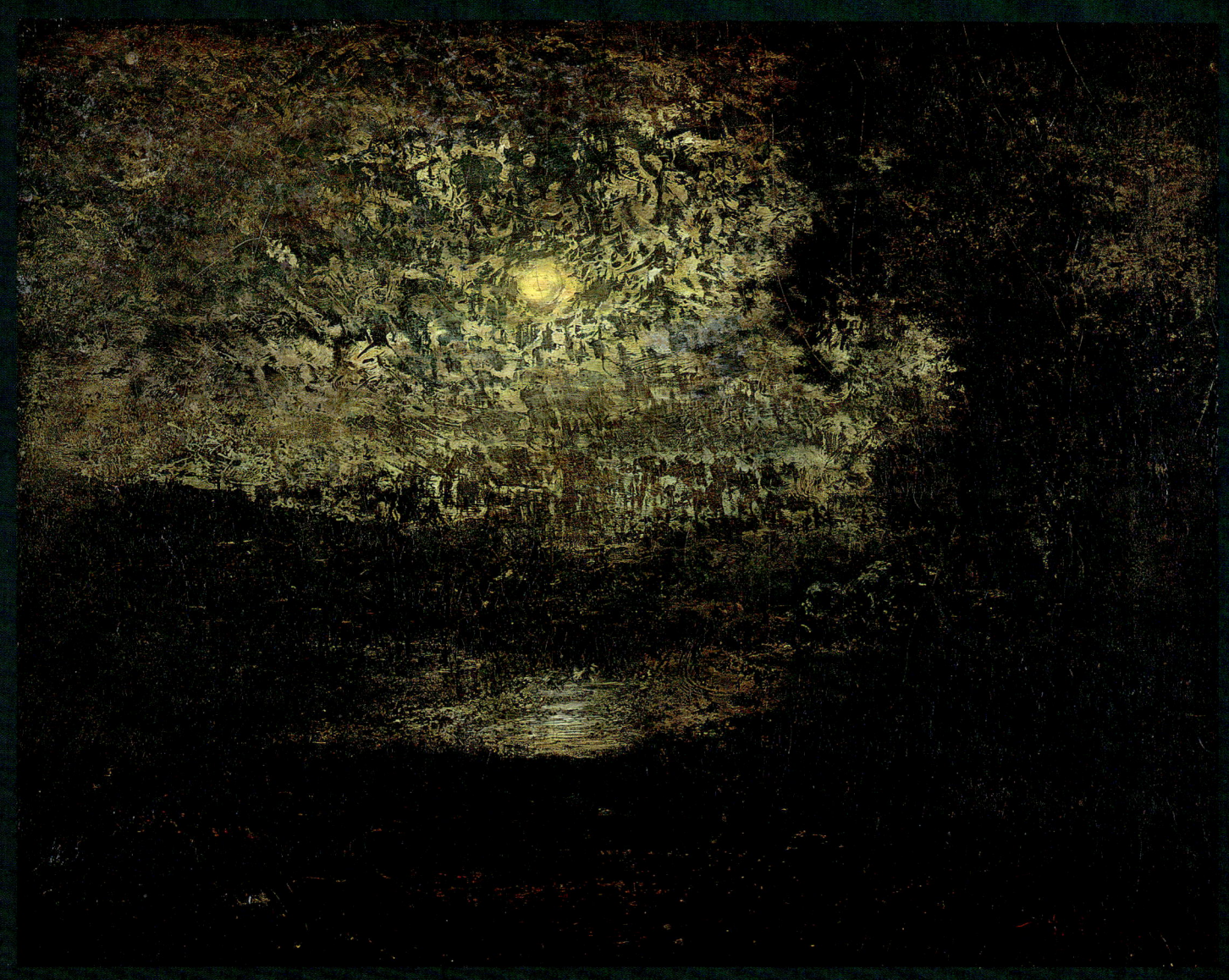

8 Moonlight, about 1880s

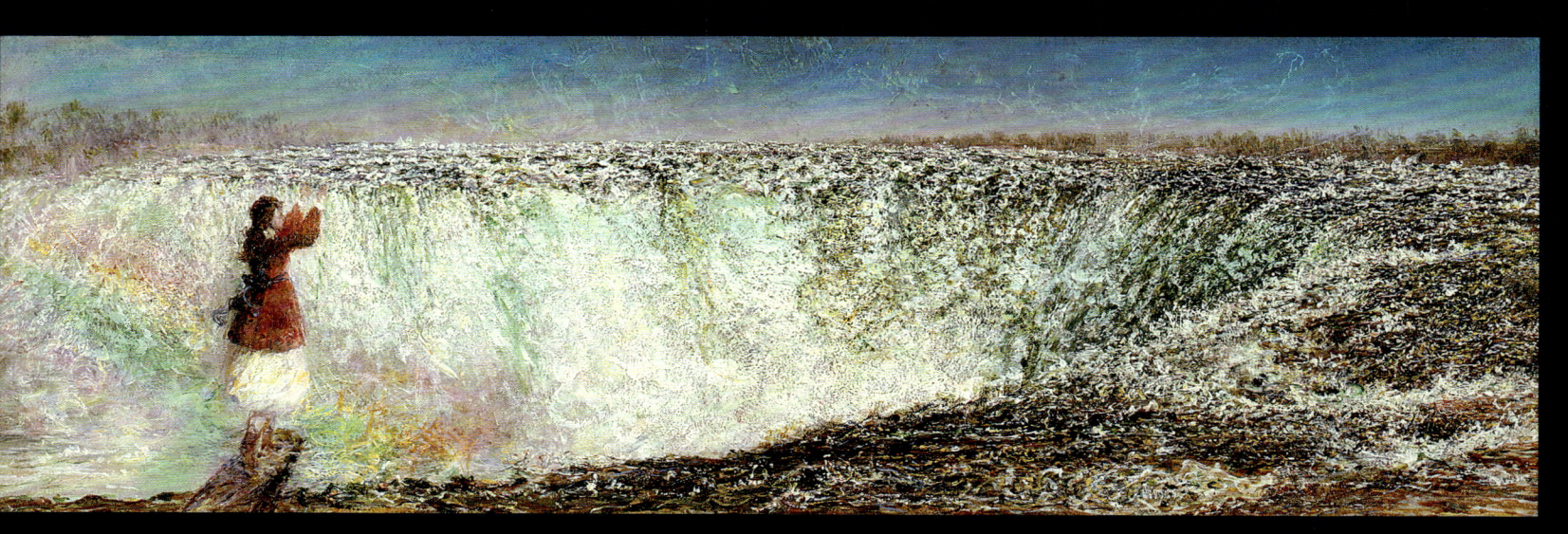

9 *Maiden in the Mist,* undated

the daring immediacy of the experience is like nothing else in the range of his work. Water as an element in the landscapes of the artist is almost always a matter of mirrored stillness or, at most, a liquid flow. Here it is tumultuous and awe inspiring. The contrast of the tumult with a placid sky is the choice of an exhilarated imagination that underlines the dramatic ritual of sacrifice.

Most of all, however, it is the figure of the girl that spells "Blakelock." Although the artist was not in any large sense a figure painter, the human presence is, even so, a constant factor in his work, almost always embedded in the texture of the scene, barely more than a colored accent. The mounted Indian that is the focus of several of the most impressive moonlights is a tiny silhouette, all but overwhelmed by nocturnal space. Again and again Blakelock populates his wooded landscapes with single figures with their backs to the observer. There is one painting of a hunter with his dog and another of a trout fisherman, both alone and almost invisible in the gloom of their surroundings. For Blakelock, the human being is a small thing in nature. The symbolism is implicit in *Maiden in the Mist* (plate 9).

We know that on the occasion of his first or second trip to the West, he went by way of Albany, which would have put him in the path of Niagara, a sight not to be missed. It can be noted that the figure hardly suggests an Indian, her gesture notwithstanding, but she does resemble the retreating figure that occurs in a number of his woodland landscapes.

Blakelock, among the painters of the last half of the nineteenth century, is exceptional in the deeply personal quality of his search for expression, a search that was largely free of tradition and convention and open to the autonomy of individual insight and, perhaps, the prescience of things to come.

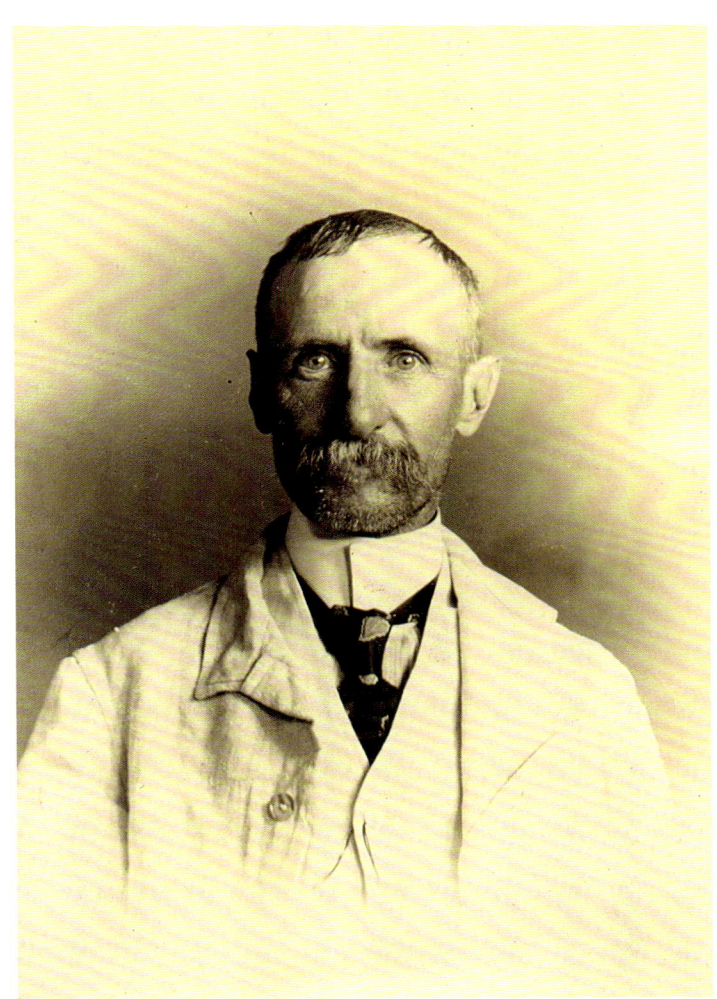

Portrait of the artist, Ralph A. Blakelock, June 25, 1901, courtesy Nebraska Blakelock Inventory, Special Collections, University of Nebraska–Lincoln Libraries.

| 25

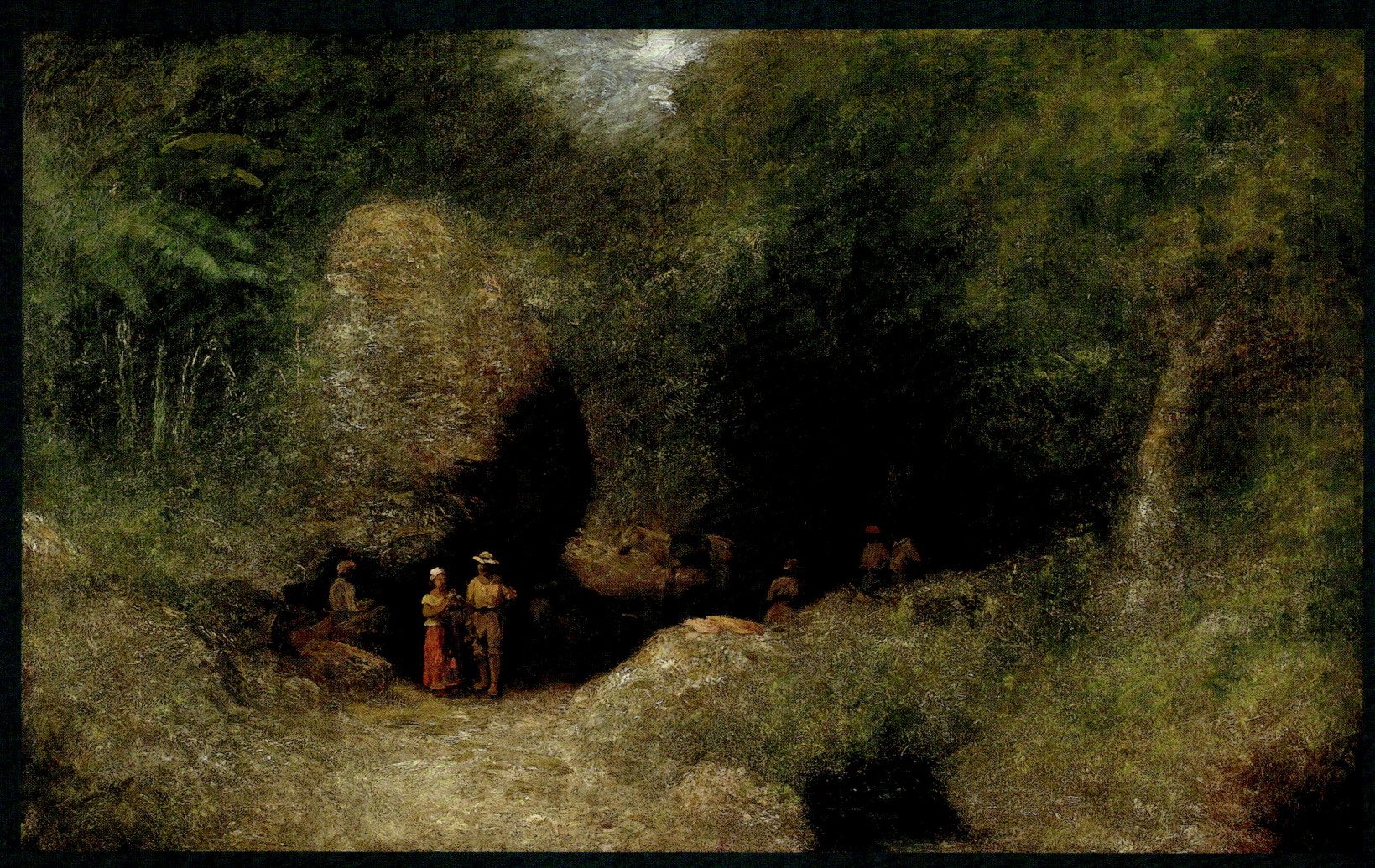

10 *The Grotto, 1880*

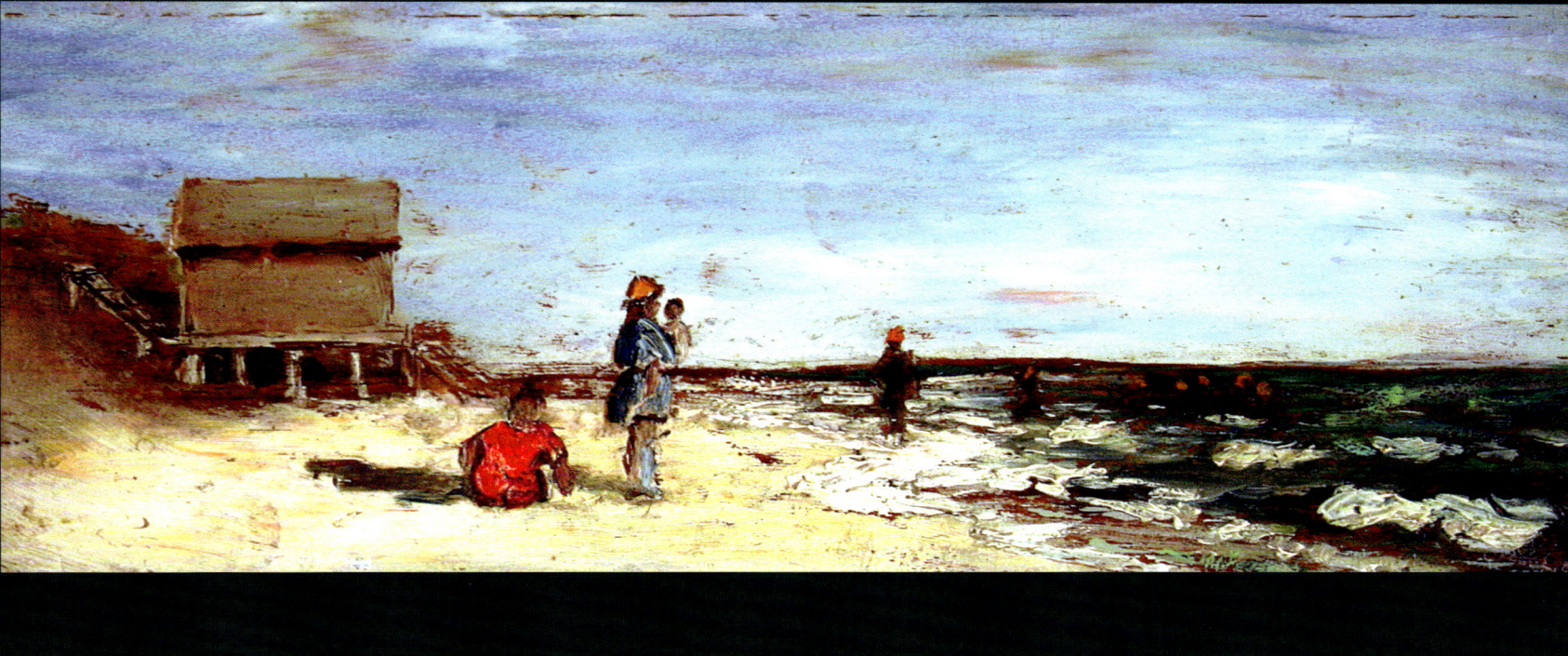

11 *Summer, undated*

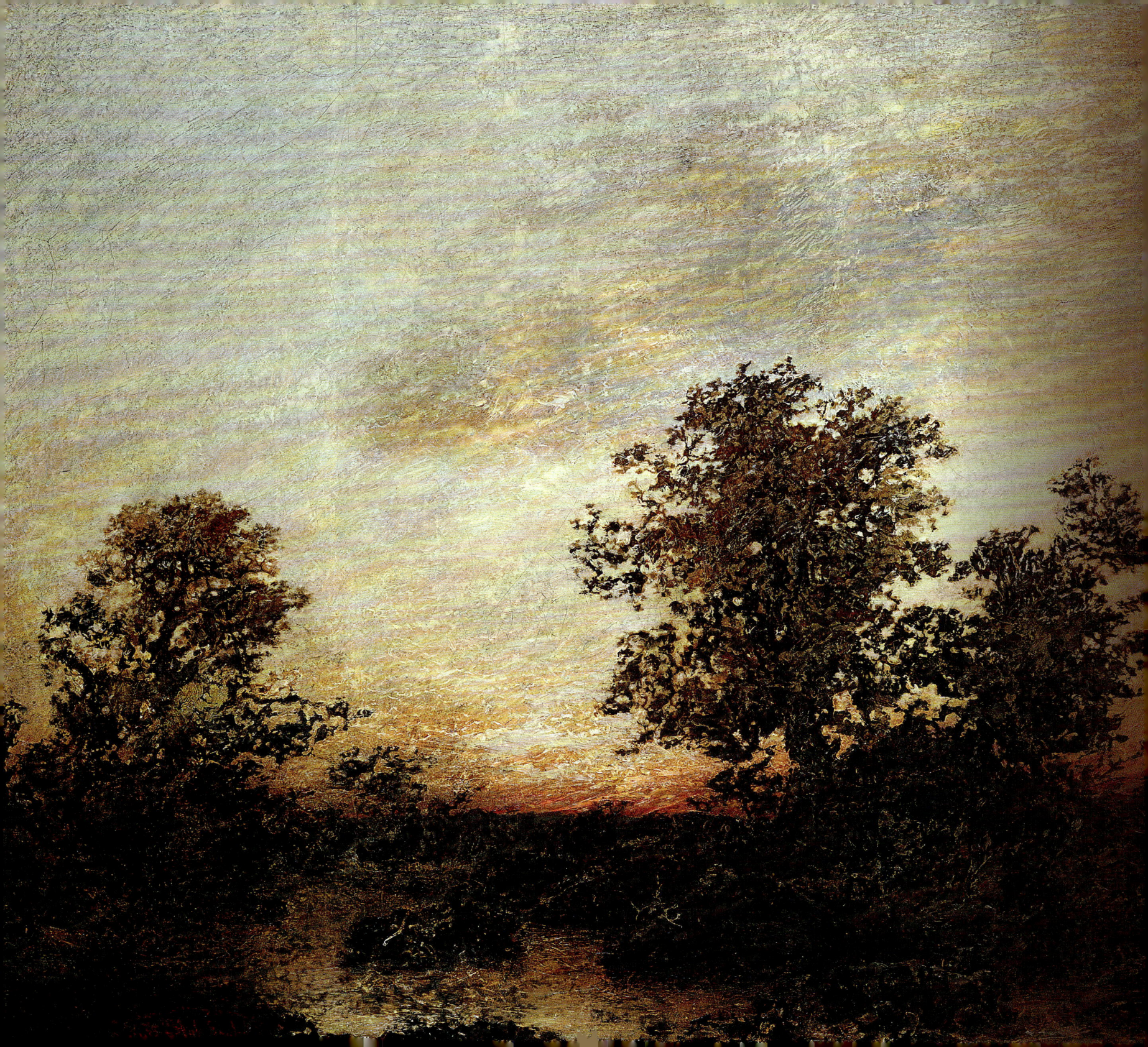

Radical Color: Blakelock in Context

MARK D. MITCHELL

Reading reviews of Ralph Albert Blakelock's paintings can be a disconcerting experience. As though a mantra, the artist's contemporaries reiterated his distinction as a colorist, and the artist reportedly believed himself "the most capable colorist since Titian."[1] Could this be the same Blakelock now enshrined in the canon of American art for his monochromatic nocturnes? The discrepancy between the critical view of Blakelock's art during his most productive years and our view today is astonishing.

This essay addresses the Blakelock of the nineteenth century, before schizophrenia largely ended his career and relegated him to an asylum from 1899 until shortly before his death in 1919. Almost immediately after his admission to the Long Island Hospital at Flatbush, his visionary nocturnes were retroactively endowed with a new aspect, "blackened with madness," in critic Sadakichi Hartmann's words.[2] Since that time, Blakelock's reputation has rested almost entirely on the artist's infirmity, his art viewed as a reflection of his insanity, despite his plea not to "harp on the plight of the man who painted [the works] for the sake of arousing interest."[3]

Among other aspects of Blakelock's work that were admired in his time but later eclipsed, color provides a useful point of entry into his art precisely because it is now so foreign to our prevailing understanding of his work today. Regrettably, a full appreciation of Blakelock's palette is no longer possible. The effects he achieved with experimental media—including the occasional use of the notoriously fugitive, petroleum-based pigment bitumen—have often proven ephemeral, irrecoverably darkening his compositions and further exacerbating Blakelock's reputation for melancholy. By focusing attention

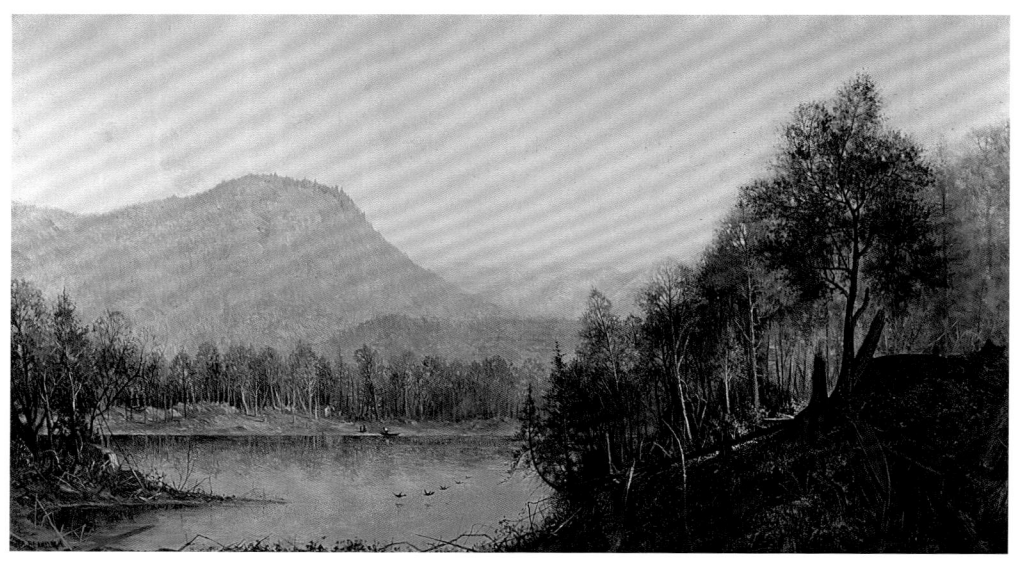

Fig. 1. RALPH ALBERT BLAKELOCK, *Catskills*, undated, oil on canvas, 20 × 36 in., formerly George F. McMurray Collection, Trinity College, Hartford, Connecticut (NBI-662.II).

on those works that do retain a sense of color and its meaning to Blakelock and his contemporaries, the opportunity arises to deepen our appreciation of his distinctive aesthetic.

RADICAL

Blakelock was an unlikely radical, a status conferred on him by critics during the 1880s. The son of a New York police officer who later became successful as a homeopathic physician, the young Blakelock benefited from a stable home, good education, and comfortable, if modest, economic means.[4] Perhaps hoping that he would follow in his father's footsteps, his family enrolled him in the Free Academy, forerunner of the City University of New York, in 1864. After three semesters of declining academic performance, however, Blakelock withdrew and turned to art. Under the guidance of self-taught landscape painter James A.

Johnson (1826–1886), Blakelock's artistic ambitions flourished. His wife, Cora, later remembered the young artist very differently from how history has recorded: "He was naturally of a bright, cheerful disposition, very affectionate and amiable and for a long time was hopeful of success."[5]

Blakelock's early aesthetic also did not predict his later style. In 1868 he began exhibiting at New York City's premier venue, the National Academy of Design's Annual Exhibition, held each spring. As do many of his earliest compositions, the work he exhibited, *Morning—near Devil's Den, White Mountains*, adopted an eastern subject such as those championed by the painters of the Hudson River School earlier in the century. By the late 1860s, however, the descriptive realism pioneered by the Hudson River School artists such as Thomas Cole (1801–1848), Asher B. Durand (1796–1886), and their disciples had begun to wane. Blakelock's early views of waterfalls, lakes, and mountains of the northeast—only a few of which are known today—demonstrate a strong, emulative foundation in Hudson River School conventions. His *Catskills* (fig. 1) illustrates the artist's allegiance to the principles expounded by Durand to art students in 1855, including close attention to detail in the foreground, naturalistic color, and gradual atmospheric recession of the distant mountain. Grounded in his renderings of specific sites and careful record of natural phenomena at the beginning of his career, Blakelock later broke with those conventions during the 1870s to seek a new, more personal mode of expression appropriate to the age.

As with the earlier generation of landscape painters that included Albert Bierstadt (1830–1902) and Thomas Moran (1837–1926), Blakelock's first journey to the American West in 1869 was a watershed that ushered in his mature style and signature subject matter.[6] Blakelock left few written documents of his career, but among those that we do have is a list of the places he visited during his journey, including travels through much of Colorado, Wyoming, Utah, and Nevada. Drawings from the period depict sites in California as well. Created after his return east later in 1869, and probably after a second trip west in 1871 or 1872, Blakelock's impressive *Indian Camp* (fig. 2) shows the artist's new subject matter, as well as the prevailing feeling of spectral mystery that characterized his mature work, while retaining the tight brushwork of his early style. The masterful play of color and light across the landscape is among the artist's finest accomplishments and marks his arrival at an aesthetic that was uniquely his own. Elliott Daingerfield (1859–1932), Blakelock's first biographer, remarked that the artist's sense of color developed out of his experience in the West as well,

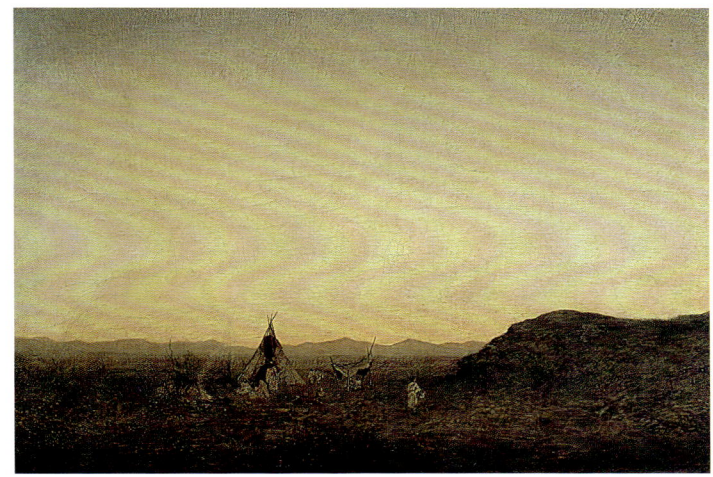

Fig. 2. RALPH ALBERT BLAKELOCK, *Indian Camp*, undated, oil on canvas, 16⅝ × 36⅝ in., Collection of Mary Ann Apicella and Jack Hollihan (NBI-204.II).

particularly in the "barbaric depth" of the colors he saw in Native American crafts and, presumably, the rich hues of the landscape itself.[7] Although the attributes that characterized Blakelock's signature works are evident in *Indian Camp*, the painting retains a sense of realism grounded in personal experience that would soon be replaced by the invented, expressive visions that were the artist's most distinctive contributions to American art.

Certain subjects and themes that Blakelock addressed during the 1870s offer an indication of his early restlessness with artistic conventions and categories. In particular, while his still lifes such as *Carnations and Zinnias* (plate 12) and *Pink Roses* (undated, private collection) retain a nominal degree of realism, they share a heightened sense of contrast and oversaturation of color that resonates more with contemporary European aesthetics than with the work of his American peers. The radiant

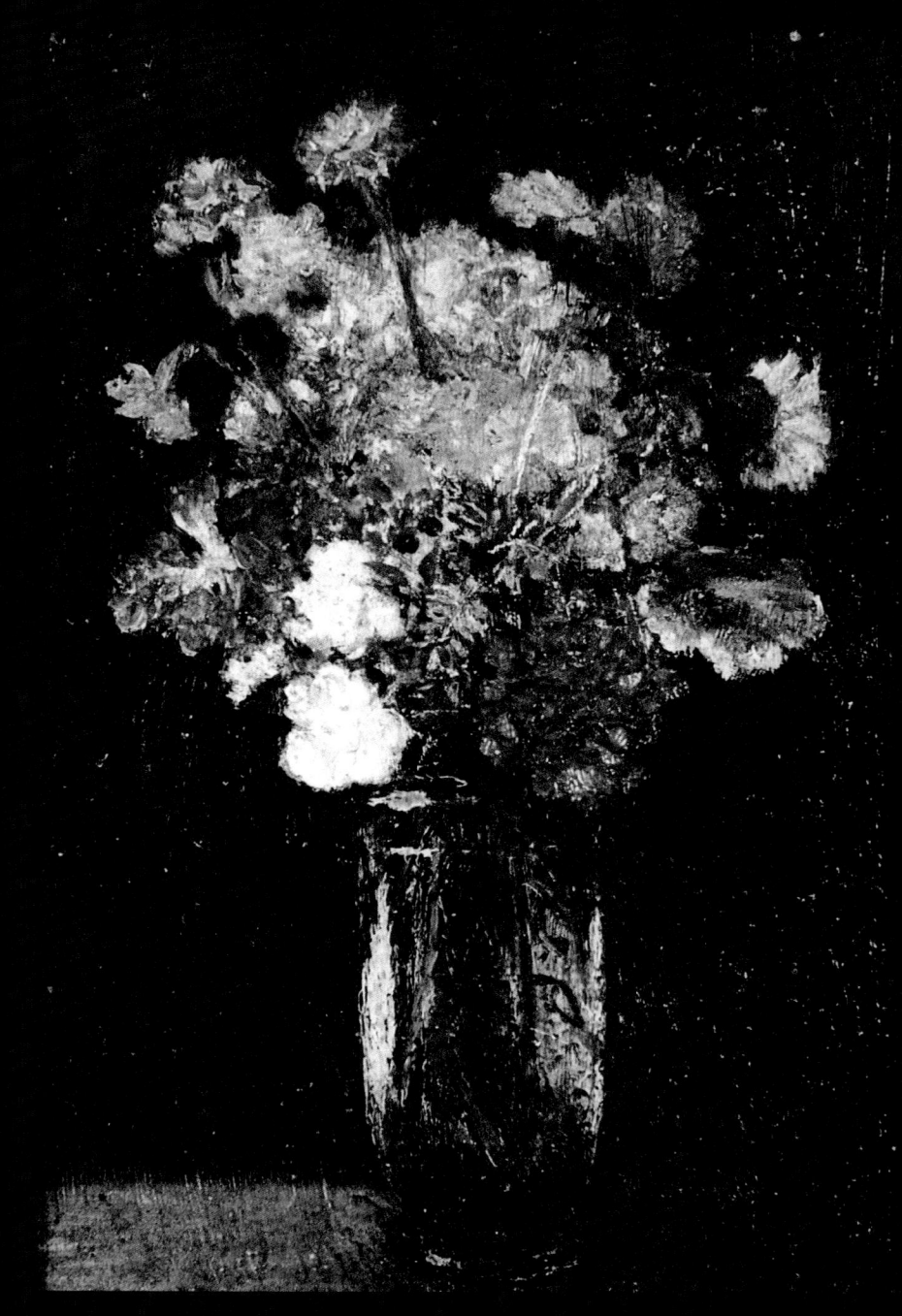

12 *Carnations and Zinnias*, about 1875–77

colors of Blakelock's flower paintings echo the brilliant luminosity of his skies, with their diffuse light filtered through the clouds and trees.

During the 1870s, Blakelock refined his approach, and by 1879 he had resolved his personal style, as documented in several dated works of that year, including both *The Captive* (Brooklyn Museum, New York) and *The Chase* (Worcester Art Museum, Massachusetts). This was also the year in which Blakelock first attracted substantive recognition in the form of a review by leading critic Charles de Kay, who admired Blakelock while decrying the poor installation of his work, which was "still possessed of sufficient inherent force to suggest that something fine is being wasted on the upper spaces of the room."[8] Because dated works are so rare in Blakelock's oeuvre, the artist's insistence on dating works in 1879 suggests a moment that merited recording, perhaps his own sense of fulfilling his artistic ambition. As one author recalled of Blakelock's self-awareness, he was "always poor and more than once was dispossessed, but he knew that he was a great artist."[9] In these compositions, Blakelock's distinctive accretion technique, still best described by Daingerfield, is in evidence:

> When the silvery ground of his picture was hard and dry, he floated upon it more forms, using thin paints much higher in quality of color; when partly dry these were flattened with a palette knife, the forms brought into relief by subtle wipings, and once more allowed to dry. This process was repeated frequently, and when the surface became gummy or over glazed, he reduced it by grinding with pumice stone. The effect of this would bring the under silver of his first *impasto* into view, and with this

for his key of gray he developed his theme, drawing with the darker and relieving with the under paint.[10]

Blakelock's palimpsestic approach has led to conflicting, even contradictory, conclusions about how long his paintings took from start to finish. Although Blakelock was capable of completing paintings in haste when necessary, his finer works required considerably more time, years rather than days. His wife offered a practical reason for the unevenness of her husband's work and regular creation of so-called potboilers: "That is easily explained," she later wrote to the dealer Robert Vose. "His best work took a long time to complete and in the meantime we had to live. Pictures were painted to keep things going. He could paint a really good picture in less time than anyone else I ever saw."[11]

To his contemporaries—as yet uninfluenced by pity—Blakelock's "best works" were a revelation. Critics who were seemingly only just becoming aware of Blakelock during the 1880s alternatively lambasted his disinterest in naturalism and heralded his abstract colorism. Little if any attention was paid to his technique, and he was quickly aligned in critics' eyes with the poetic aesthetic of Albert Pinkham Ryder (1847–1917), a relationship that historians have largely dismissed for lack of documentation.[12] Irrespective of whether the artists were friends or even acquaintances, both must have been aware of their alignment in the press. In 1893, a critic from the *Boston Evening Transcript* remarked on their shared standing as "[t]wo strange Manhattan geniuses . . . who are not usually appreciated at their true worth, except in certain circles; they are originals, with imagination, color, and more real art spirit than the fashionable and blatant posers whose pictures figure in the collections of the mushroom millionaires."[13] Although reviewers were rarely so sympathetic, they generally agreed that on the basis of color alone Blakelock, like Ryder, contributed a fresh perspective to an art world dominated by convention.

The deeply expressive, personal aspect of Blakelock's mature works is at once what makes them so compelling and what opens them to oversimplification. Frederick W. Morton was among the first to compare Blakelock's work with the writing of Edgar Allan Poe, "the man of gloomy fancies," in its degree of personal involvement.[14] That comparison is apt, as it encourages the type of lingering study and appreciation of layered metaphors found in both men's work. Blakelock's technique— the accumulation of experience, form, color, and feeling over long periods of time—imbues his art with a sense of underlying deliberation and allusion. As Morton observed, the artist "dreamed strange dreams and told them in remarkable color schemes."[15] Morton was by no means the last to describe the dreamlike quality of Blakelock's art. Art historian Lloyd Goodrich used similarly evocative terms to describe how the artist was "haunted by the forest, the primeval background of early America, with its savage inhabitants, its mystery and terror."[16] Indeed, the otherworldly radiance of Blakelock's great Indian encampments, twilights, and nocturnes elicits unease. The molten effect of color and medium in his *Indian Encampment at Sunset* (fig. 3) upends the symbolism of Native American cultures as innocent and suggests instead the kind of supernatural vision that reappears in many of Blakelock's most coloristic scenes. As Goodrich remarked, "[i]n a day when most of his generation had their eyes fixed on Europe, he almost alone remained aware of this ancient element in the American consciousness."[17] Goodrich's observation is striking and offers a

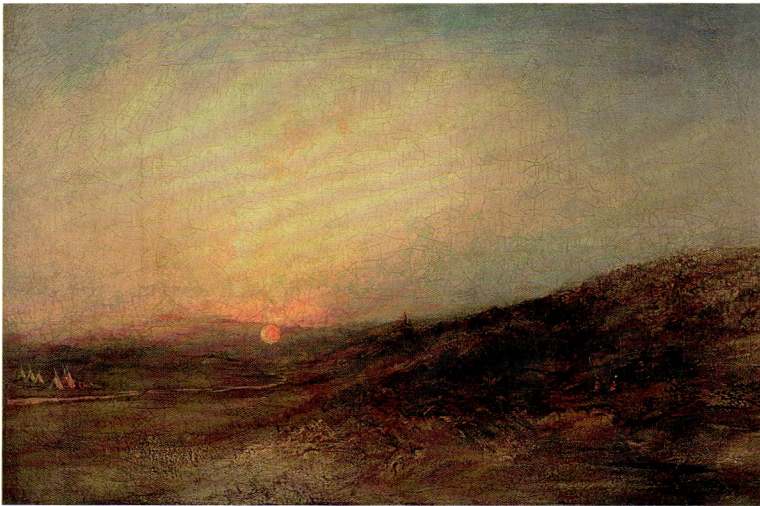

Fig. 3. RALPH ALBERT BLAKELOCK, *Indian Encampment at Sunset*, about 1880–1884, oil on canvas, 20 × 30 in., Collection of Julie and Lawrence Salander.

key to understanding the unique aspects of Blakelock's art to which we will return.

Blakelock's personality was equally engaging. As one anonymous critic wrote with evangelical zeal in 1890:

He was a man of short stature and a spare frame, and he was surrounded by works which had the fibre of Titanism in them. Out of the gray-blue eyes he turned upon me shone the soul of a poet. His voice had a ring of music in it, and his lean hand, which he extended in cordial greeting to the unaccustomed stranger, the thrill of a living soul. For a moment the extraordinary vitality of the man seemed to broaden and brighten the room, invaded through its skylight by the November fog. Then, that which the man had produced, warmed the room into a glow of quite another life. . . . Down in this dingy well in Tenth street, so solitary that the very starved mice in the wainscot were more sociable and not much less fortunate in worldly things than he, the soul that sang within him kept him alive.[18]

The meeting described must have happened in 1884, the only year in which Blakelock is known to have had a studio in the celebrated Tenth Street Studio Building, a moment of relative ease in the artist's career.[19]

Married in 1877, before his income could sustain a family, Blakelock soon settled into a pattern of financial difficulty. The Blakelocks had nine children, eight of whom survived to adulthood. The burden of caring for his growing family weighed heavily on the artist, who famously sold his works with greater and greater haste and at ever-decreasing prices as his family grew. Despite the support of several committed patrons and friends, the birth of his ninth child in September 1899 coincided with Blakelock's final breakdown and his confinement to an asylum following at least a decade of intermittent struggle with mental illness.[20] Biographers often remark on the fact that the artist's later delusions involved having great wealth, which he had so pointedly lacked.

The commonly held belief that Blakelock was unknown and unappreciated during his lifetime, however, strains credulity. Over the course of his career he worked in two of the leading and most important studio buildings in New York, Tenth Street and the Sherwood Building (although he borrowed, rather than rented, space in the latter for much of his time there). Moreover, the public exhibition of his art at key venues and its frequent mention in the columns of influential critics led to sales to several well-known patrons. Most artists suffered from far greater neglect than Blakelock, and yet the perception that the artist was neglected by his contemporaries persists, perhaps induced by the events of his later life. The artist's financial hardships also undoubtedly fueled that perception, but Blakelock might partly be to blame for his family's struggles as their expenditures outstripped their income. His sense of his own prodigious talent might have led him to overreach his situation, which in turn only deepened his distress as he turned to his patrons in desperation and painted lesser works in haste, swamping the market for his own better productions. In the end, the artist's tragic struggles were in part the product of hubris. Certainly reviews and other published accounts of Blakelock's early career do not suggest the degree of critical neglect that we expect a radical to suffer.

Blakelock was a painter's painter. His commitment to his unique, deeply personal vision offered a source of inspiration to colleagues. As a technician, he was an innovator and suffered the consequences. Many of his works have darkened or discolored beyond repair. Critics and early biographers pointed to Blakelock's ephemeral media to make separate points, either to diminish his standing among American artists or to belittle his technical skills. The alchemy of art is not always rewarded, however, and that process of experimenting with, testing, and thinking about materials was integral to Blakelock's distinctive approach and endeared him to colleagues who could, according to one report, purchase "Blakelock Varnish" in art supply stores.[21]

Collectors, however, often prefer less ambition in the artists whose works they collect, and while Blakelock garnered the devoted support of numerous artists and a few collectors during his career, relatively few wealthy patrons followed. His artist-friend and devoted advocate Harry Watrous (1857–1940) not only bought approximately thirty of Blakelock's works but also lent Blakelock his Sherwood studio for several years. At major exhibitions, Blakelock listed his works for sale at several hundred dollars, although his success in selling at that price is undocumented. His more frequent and better-known sales were in the range of twenty-five dollars or even less. At the nadir of his struggles, Blakelock reportedly sold a group of thirty-three paintings for a hundred dollars, an event that may have precipitated his decline.

After Blakelock was institutionalized, the secondary market for his works soared, peaking in 1916 when his *Brook by Moonlight* was purchased for the Toledo Museum of Art for twenty thousand dollars. (The artist had originally sold it for five hundred dollars.) The history of Blakelock's reputation in the twentieth century, including the vast market for forgeries and the victimization of the artist and his family during that period, only extended the tragedy of his later life. Those chapters, which have been the primary focus of Blakelock scholarship in recent years, are beyond the scope of this essay.[22] Blakelock benefited from none of the acclaim that followed his institutionalization, all of which adopted the reverent tone of a eulogy and was phrased in the past tense. Today the "unknown" Blakelock describes virtually the whole of his life and career before he entered the asylum in 1899.

COLOR

Blakelock's use of color had several resonances that were noted in the press to distinguish his art from that of other vision-ary artists of his day—including Ryder, Homer Dodge Martin (1836–1897), and Alexander Helwig Wyant (1836–1892)—as well as from the precedent of French Barbizon painting and the contemporary tonalist style. There are two reasons to lend added weight to contemporary critical estimates of Blakelock's art. The first is the scarcity of Blakelock's known writings, which by and large echo the terms in which critics described his work. These reviews, along with early biographies by people who knew the artist, offer the closest equivalent to a statement by the artist about his approach. The second reason to study the reviews is that their authors observed Blakelock's art shortly after its creation and before time affected his palette. The continuing study of Blakelock's pigments provides ever more information about what his art might have originally looked like, but reviewers of the period saw the works as we cannot. Their emphasis on the themes of music, mood, and faith frames Blakelock's art in a new constellation and suggests promising avenues for future research.

Music was Blakelock's second passion. Colors were not words to Blakelock, as they were to George Inness (1825–1894), but musical notes.[23] The author of the artist's biographical entry in *Appleton's Cyclopedia* observed that Blakelock "has endeavored to bring out the beauty of a painting by the treatment of color, until it seems to flow upon the senses, as some melody."[24] In his paintings, Blakelock fused his appreciation for music and his practice of art. As an anonymous critic observed in *The Artist* in 1901, Blakelock "is a musician as well as a painter, and makes the twin arts interpret each other."[25]

Several anecdotes of Blakelock's passion for music recur in contemporary accounts. His neighbor Albert Schoch, reportedly "a musician of unusual ability," remembered that "it was while listening one evening to the *Moonlight Sonata* that Blakelock suddenly rose from his rigid pose of fascination, and rushed across the street [to his own home] to put on canvas his first moonlight picture, which he brought over to his friend with a triumphant smile, the paint still wet, but his inspiration fulfilled."[26] The Museum of Fine Arts in Boston owns a work by that title (ca. 1892), suggesting that it may be the very object that Schoch saw. The translation of music into painting is a consistent theme in early accounts of Blakelock's art that hinges on his dramatic colorism, as he found range and nuance in his accumulated layers of overlapping, semitransparent hues.

In one of the few survey texts to mention the depth of Blakelock's colorism, the art historian John Wilmerding addressed the interactions of color ranges in his work, observing that "his colour was highly original, most often structured around dark blues, greens, and blacks, in counterpoint with the yellows and whites."[27] The musical counterpoint that Wilmerding described is most often a contrast between earth and sky, harmony and melody. Blakelock's skies throughout the two decades of his mature career propel the artist's lyricism. *After Sundown* (plate 13) offers a luminous account of Blakelock's accomplishment, incorporating a range of colors from the horizon to the ethereal upper sky. The water below harmonizes with the sky, bringing the lighter palette above into the deeper tones of the shadowed foreground. As Blakelock observed, "there is music in a good painting as well as other qualities."[28]

Blakelock reversed the conventional relationship between art and music. Any number of artists of the nineteenth century proclaimed their discovery of music in the landscape, but Blakelock found the landscape in music. He remarked to one critic that "he could sit at the piano, and improvising as the spirit moved him work out a theme for a painting in his best vein and with absolute fidelity to the truth of nature."[29] That practice opposed Durand's dictum that the artist must go first to nature, as well as critic John Ruskin's mandate that nature be observed in every detail in order to find meaning. Nevertheless, the invocation of the term "truth of nature" echoes the principles of earlier American landscape painting. Despite the visionary nature of his later aesthetic, Blakelock retained his commitment to the idea of "truthful" representation. In his case, however, "truth" meant not only the devotional revelation of a divine spirit—a subject to which we will return—but also the viewer's ability to share in universal meaning, which he believed to be intrinsic to music.

In the age of composer Richard Wagner, whom Blakelock admired, music and the sister arts drew closer than they had since the baroque. The 1880s and 1890s were the age of symbolism in Europe, a cultural moment in which creative minds sought common ground between poetry, music, and visual art. Perhaps partly from a desire to immure Blakelock within the borders of the United States, rendering him a uniquely American genius independent of foreign influence, biographers and art historians have often ignored Blakelock's affinity with symbolism. Picking up the thread from the romantics from earlier in the century, symbolist artists such as Emile Bernard (1868–1941) and Paul Gauguin (1848–1903) reintroduced subjectivity to art. Blakelock's abstract color provides an important link to European symbolism that merits a more complete discussion, not least because it distinguishes Blakelock's work from that of his American contemporaries, notably his more literary peers.

Ryder's romanticism was more conventional than Blakelock's. Ryder's *Siegfried and the Rhinemaidens* illustrates an

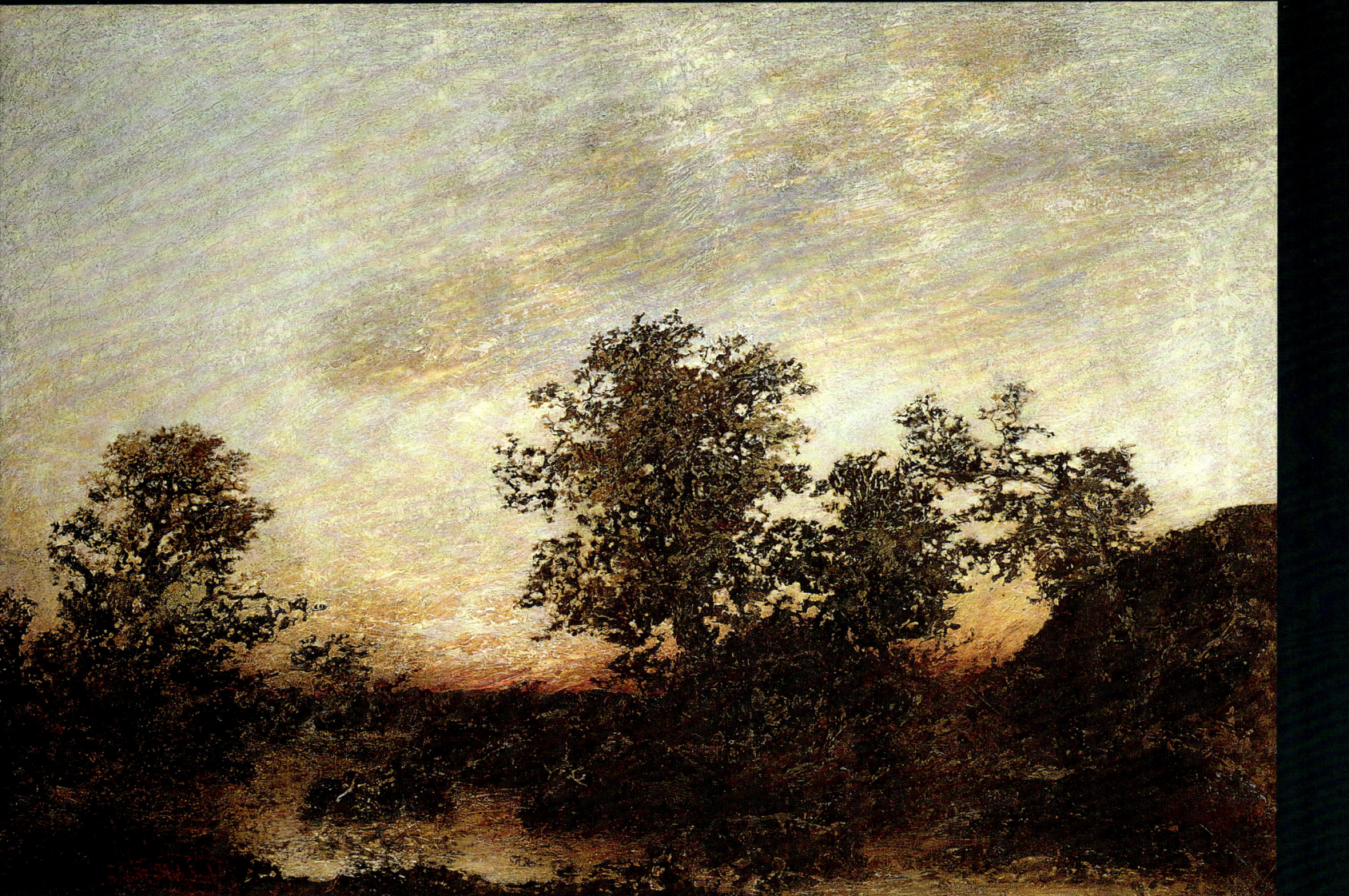

awareness of Wagner and his passion in music; it is one of the composer's most celebrated works. And yet, like most of Ryder's works, it is illustrative, tied irrevocably to its particular source. Ryder sought a visual analogue of Wagner's music, and he created an impressive composition, but it is one that differs in kind from Blakelock's work, which is primarily self-referential. Blakelock translated music's interpretive system, particularly its sensory impact on the listener, rather than any single piece of music. (His *Moonlight Sonata* is a rare, if not unique, exception.)

Contrasting Blakelock's *Pegasus* (plate 7) with Ryder's *Pegasus* (Worcester Art Museum, Massachusetts) is instructive, as it illustrates the difference between Ryder's narrative approach and Blakelock's evocation of a similar subject.[30] Ryder's figures are fully conceived and dominate the landscape, whereas Blakelock's leaping horse appears to dissolve within a highly abstracted landscape of textures and colors in which the brilliant white figures rise to a symbolic or spiritual level. Much of Ryder's oeuvre reflects such literary narratives or operatic transliteration, as in his *Christ Appearing to Mary, Jonah, The Tempest, Macbeth and the Witches,* and his celebrated *Flying Dutchmen,* also likely based on Wagner.[31] Perhaps the most direct analogy between the two artists' works is found in Ryder's moonlight marines and Blakelock's moonlight landscapes. Despite the obvious shared subjectivity, however, Ryder's approach remains more directly tied to the romantic tradition of the early nineteenth century, including the works of Théodore Géricault (1791–1824), than do Blakelock's more contemplative evocations, which introduce chromatic and textural experiments.

Blakelock's colorism also differed in kind from the techniques of the American tonalist painters with whom he is often associated. Inness, Thomas Wilmer Dewing (1851–1938), Dwight Tryon (1849–1925), and, most famously, James McNeill Whistler (1834–1903) were the pillars of tonalism, and their work is linked by a unity of hue, thin application, and soft focus. Whistler's use of musical terms such as "symphony," "harmony," and "variations" in his titles offers the strongest link between his art and music. Despite that shared interest, however, Whistler and the tonalists only lightly reinterpreted the techniques of impressionism in their generally wistful, leisure subjects. Their lyric, poetic form of refinement and gentility bore little resemblance to Blakelock's intensity and personal investment, a split that is consistent with contemporary critical views. During the period, observers clearly did not associate Blakelock with the tonalists; they viewed him as an outsider instead, and scholars still limit the tonalists' influence on him to the "general."[32] Ultimately, Blakelock's dense palette and dramatic light effects bore little resemblance to tonalist aesthetics, and his association with their work in later years was inaccurate.

Critics nevertheless used similar musical terminology to characterize Blakelock's art and that of his contemporaries. How then are we to differentiate when the same term is used to describe such different aesthetics? The answer lies in context. Just as the term *poetic* was used to describe nearly every American landscapist of the mid-nineteenth century, so *musical* was employed during the later century. Both poetry and music, however, have a stylistic range that is equal to painting. A *musical* painting was one that provided a sense of allusion beyond direct observation. In Blakelock's case, however, finding visual inspiration in the aural went beyond a general sense of allusion. It also influenced his techniques and materials, an approach documented by contemporary reviews. Critics linked his music to his color, anticipating a modernist leap that color theorist Maud Miles later summarized: "The truest parallel that I can conceive between direct light rays of color and music would be to lay aside all attempts to represent objects either in a natural or conventional way, in using the color. To simply use color as music, might prove a genuinely new art."[33] The critic Charles Caffin elaborated, reporting that Blakelock "worked out for his own use a chromatic scale of color equivalent to that of music."[34] Blakelock's palette can be vivid, but it is more often simply imaginary, providing the primary vehicle through which the artist differentiated his work from his contemporaries, as he transformed color into an expressive rather than descriptive medium. By describing his work as musical with respect to its color, critics could address his visionary abstraction from nature, for which they as yet lacked a vocabulary.

Mood is the second aspect by which critics characterized Blakelock's colorism, and this dimension highlights the artist's unique romanticism. Critics generally agreed with Frederick W. Morton that Blakelock's "dreamy, mystical, poetic turn of mind prompted his subjects, and gave his canvases the moody characteristics that mark them."[35] Color is often considered the medium of emotion in art, and by pointing to color as Blakelock's leading quality, critics aligned his work with emotion and the romantic tradition. Romanticism does not translate into insanity, however, even with the clear correlation in later authors' views between the depth of feeling exhibited in Blakelock's work and his mental illness. Blakelock employed color selectively. Its emotive emphasis drew attention as a distinguishing trait, distancing his art in contemporary eyes from the earlier Barbizon school, with which he was most often compared. Critics regularly associated his works with Barbizon aesthetics, but they just as regularly added the caveat that his colorism distinguished his work from the earlier models of Théodore Rousseau (1812–1867) , Narcisse-Virgile Diaz de la Peña (1808–1876), and, in particular, Adolphe Monticelli (1824–1886).[36]

Blakelock was by no means the only American artist to turn inward in search of meaningful expression following the conclusion of the Civil War in 1865. In fact, psychology became a popular science as Americans struggled with the lingering sense of loss and displacement that the war created. Blakelock's mature landscapes contributed to an expressive vein in American realist art that vied with the more cheerful impressionist scenes of upper-class ease and idleness depicted by artists such as William Merritt Chase (1849–1916) and Childe Hassam (1859–1935). Blakelock's frequent depiction of Native American subjects added to a sense of distance and separation that recalled the nation's early history of discovery and encounter with Indian peoples. During the Civil War, artists such as Frederic Edwin Church (1826–1900), who was a friend of Blakelock's teacher James Johnson, adopted vibrant colorism over the undeveloped wilderness as a metaphor for the nation's crisis in his celebrated *Twilight in the Wilderness* (1860, Cleveland Museum of Art). Two decades later, Blakelock's vibrant *Indian Encampment at Sunset* (fig. 3) distills the war's tragic legacy. Although Blakelock was too young to serve in the military for most of the war, he was certainly old enough to observe its effects and reckon with its impact.

Indian Encampment at Sunset is an impressive document of Blakelock's colorism in its mature phase. Daingerfield remarked that Blakelock depicted only two "phases of nature," twilight and moonlight, and the former was naturally the more vividly coloristic.[37] In this composition, a tapering stream arcs from the village at the left edge of the composition to the sun dipping into the effulgent atmosphere near the horizon. The village is shown at a distance, dwarfed by the looming dark hillside at the right, which pushes both the dramatic sun and the modest encampment off center. Picturesque asymmetry was another signature feature of Blakelock's mature aesthetic, although it is subtle here. A tiny figure stands midway along the hillside, almost lost in the luster of the sun's brilliance. The artist has lowered the horizon line, amplifying the expanse of sky and therefore its color. The composition does not suggest conflict or bloodshed in the manner of Church's earlier twilight but offers instead a feeling of nostalgia. Blakelock's palette is brilliant but soft. Whereas Church emphasized the contrast of brilliant, saturated color against the darkening sky, Blakelock's orange, yellow, and teal interpenetrate and transition gradually. The small group of tepees appears vulnerable in number as well as in their minute size in proportion to the expansive landscape. Unlike the sublime, impassioned effect of Church's *Twilight,* Blakelock's *Encampment* employs his rich palette to a more meditative end.

As Blakelock entered his professional maturity during the late 1870s, critics primarily compared his art with the French Barbizon school. Blakelock had never traveled abroad, so his knowledge of the Barbizon painters had to come from visits to exhibitions and collections that included their work. By the 1880s, however, the prevailing aesthetic of American landscape had shifted squarely toward impressionism, which Blakelock's work never resembled. Instead he gravitated toward the personal style of the earlier Barbizon painters for its dramatic contrasts and escape from modern urban life. Led by Rousseau,

the Barbizon painters had sought new inspiration in the rural landscape during the 1830s and throughout the mid-century. They sought *truth* in the landscape as much as their British and American peers, yet they undertook their research in a more personal vein that distinguished each artist in the group from the others. Unlike the Hudson River School, whose artists shared similar conventions and often identical views, the Barbizon painters developed their own singular manners, an approach for which Blakelock himself would later be criticized as his own imitator.[38] Nevertheless, the emotive style of the Barbizon painters clearly appealed to Blakelock, and it offered him an alternative to the more communal approach of the Hudson River School.

Critics often associated Blakelock's art with Rousseau and Diaz, but most often he was known as the American Monticelli, a lesser-known Barbizon landscapist who also reportedly suffered from mental illness. That attribute is clearly the primary reasoning behind the association of the two artists' work by early biographers, and yet the association has endured. Admirers of Monticelli have called him "a crucial pioneer in the evolution of painting in 19th-century France," who influenced both Paul Cézanne (1839–1906) and Vincent van Gogh (1853–1890).[39] Monticelli's career offers a little-known link between the late eighteenth-century rococo's flights of fancy and later nineteenth-century symbolism. The connections with Blakelock extend to the artists' shared impressions from music, comparable techniques, and romanticism. Monticelli's virtuosic style offers a significant precedent for Blakelock's art, as in Monticelli's countryside scenes such as *A Dream of Woods and Sunlight* (fig. 4), which are often so heavily textured that their subjects compete in level of visual interest with the surface of the paint

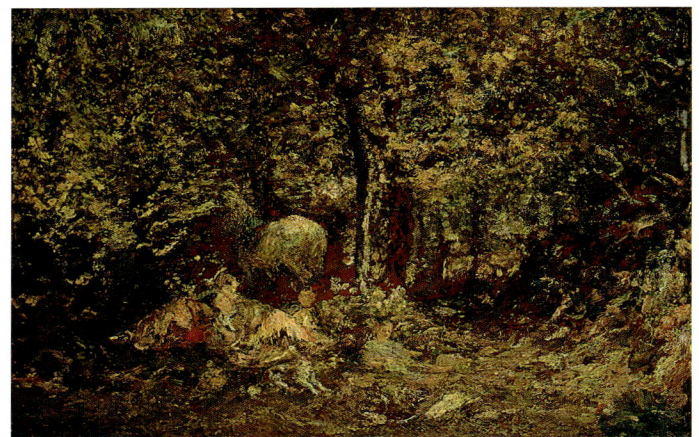

Fig. 4. Adolphe Monticelli (1824–1886), *A Dream of Woods and Sunlight*, about 1869, oil on canvas, 15 × 23 in., Corcoran Gallery of Art, Washington, DC.

itself. Monticelli's work was known in New York through dealer Daniel Cottier, and Blakelock must have seen it.[40] Monticelli's influence on Blakelock, however, is documented by stylistic and personal affinity alone.

In his signature *fêtes champêtres*, Monticelli successfully modernized a classic theme and incorporated it into a personal blend of more recent techniques pioneered by Eugène Delacroix (1798–1863) and Diaz. Blakelock's approach to the Indian encampment echoed Monticelli's project, as did his self-identification as the inheritor of the mantle of the great Venetian Renaissance colorists. Monticelli's innovations of the 1860s, following his training with Diaz during the mid-1850s, provide a precedent for Blakelock that bridges the gap between his work and that of the Barbizon painters.

A crucial area in which Blakelock does not compare easily with Monticelli, however, is his faith. Critics remarked on a sense of mysticism in Blakelock's work as the third dimension of his colorism, but doubtless few were aware of his association with Swedenborgian spirituality in particular. Similarly, studies of Blakelock's art and career have until recently almost entirely overlooked his specific faith, and even those treatments remain preliminary, with a great deal more work still to be undertaken.[41]

Biblical themes were common enough in the art of Blakelock's contemporaries, but he eschewed them. Instead he favored more discrete devotional references, such as those found in his ethereal *The Three Trees* (fig. 5), which revisits Rembrandt's vision of the crucifixion set in natural terms. To Rembrandt's theme Blakelock added a lighthouse, visible across the bay in the middleground through veils of atmosphere. The analogy between the guiding beacon of the lighthouse and the moonlight visible through the lattice of the largest tree is clear yet understated. The effulgent light and hazy atmosphere amplify the painting's spiritual feeling, as does the halo of blue sky encircling the trees. Embedding spiritual subtexts within color choices was consistent with Blakelock's faith and was remarkably apparent to contemporary critics who were accustomed to finding religious undertones in depictions of the American landscape.

Recent scholarship on Inness—who was not only a fellow devotee of Swedenborgianism but also Blakelock's neighbor in Orange, New Jersey—has greatly enhanced our appreciation of Blakelock's faith. Founded by the eighteenth-century scientist and theologian Emanuel Swedenborg, the Swedenborgian Church espouses the coexistence of physical and spiritual worlds, with objects in each having a direct, corresponding equivalent in the other. As scholar Sally Promey first discussed

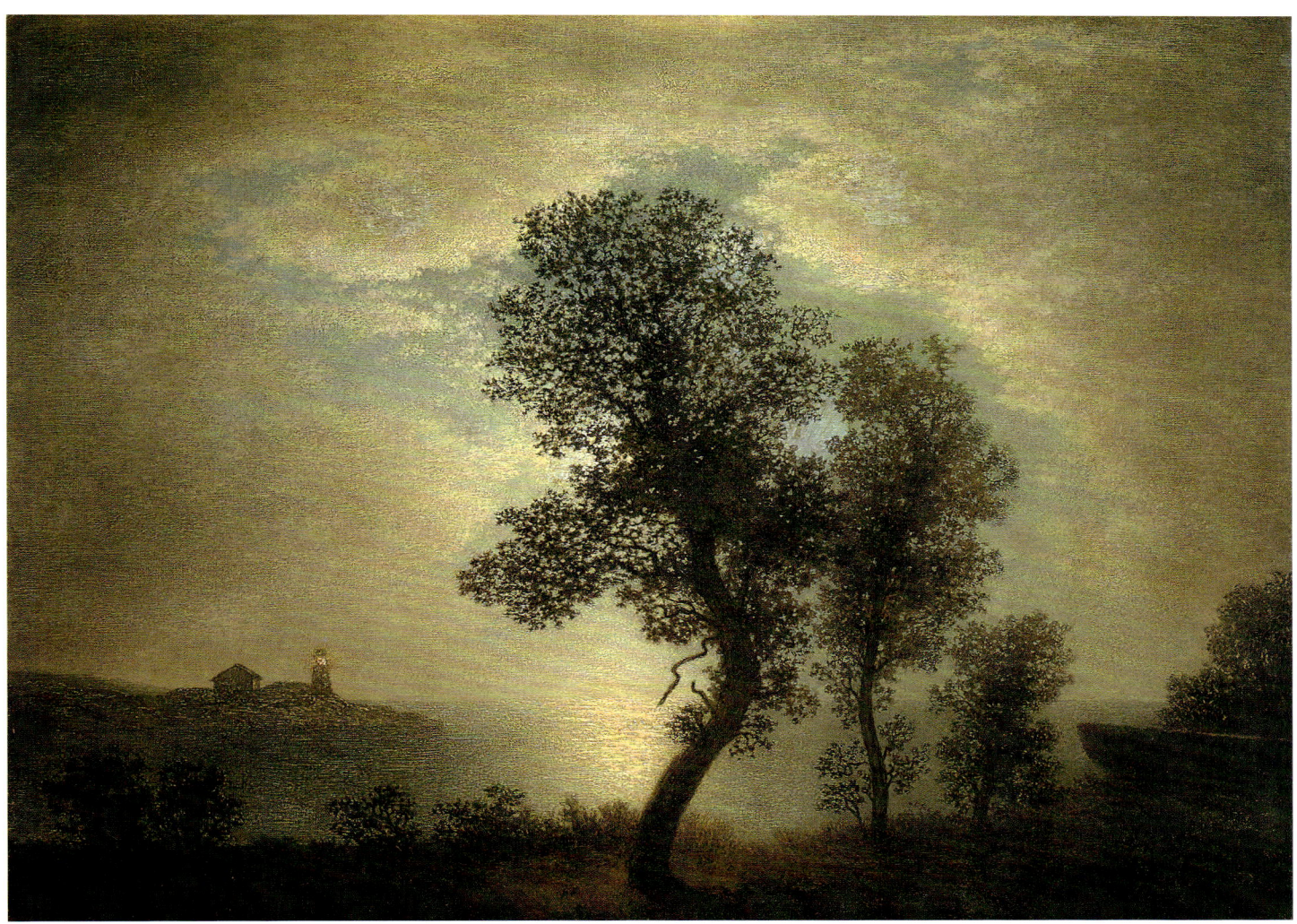

Fig. 5. Ralph Albert Blakelock, *The Three Trees*, about 1885, oil on canvasboard, 22 × 30 in., Hirshhorn Museum and Sculpture Garden, Washington, DC (NBI-601).

in a pioneering article on Inness's color use, color held important symbolic power for Swedenborgians. Inness published his thoughts on the subject in an 1867 article entitled "Colors and Their Correspondences." Returning to Blakelock's composition, the blue sky that silhouettes the trees adopts new meaning in light of Inness's remark that "blue presents an idea of what is spiritual and appears like something intangible."[42] Although it is difficult to equate Inness's theory of colors with Blakelock's given the differences between their aesthetics, the overlap in their views is suggestive. Moreover, as Promey points out, even "slight change in value or hue could change the significance of the correspondences suggested."[43] Their goal was not, however, to transcribe a single, programmatic symbolism that could only be interpreted by an informed viewer. Instead, Blakelock, like Inness, sought to convey the feeling of an animating, spiritual presence behind natural forms. According to Blakelock, "the laws of the art of painting are the laws of the creator, as to expression, color, form, unity, harmony, height, depth, tone."[44]

Landscape for Inness, as for Blakelock, was increasingly an internal, symbolic form. As Eugene Taylor has remarked, "when we try to look at one of his landscapes from a Swedenborgian point of view, as Inness in all likelihood himself saw it when he looked at the canvas, the picture ceases to be for us a mere depiction of a scene in nature and becomes instead a representation of one of the artist's own interior states of consciousness."[45] Taylor's observation eloquently summarizes Blakelock's approach to landscape, filtered through memory and inspired by musical or other abstract suggestion. By liberating color from its role in describing objects in nature and instead using it to evoke an interior experience and meaning, he was able to project a sense of "nature" into his imagined landscapes. Perhaps the most notable element of his landscapes is how far west he traveled in search of subject matter suitable as a medium for his internal visions.

FRONTIERS

As we revisit Blakelock's art, we must address two recurring frontiers, one literal and one metaphorical. The literal frontier is external, found at the edge of American civilization in the West where Blakelock set many of his landscapes. The other is internal, at the limit of the conscious mind. Over and over in Blakelock's art, we encounter frontiers that parallel or amplify these two primary thresholds, including his elegant, silhouetted screens of tree limbs spread across the picture plane between viewer and landscape; his twilight subjects set between day and night; and his renderings of shanties found at the city's outer edge. Moreover, Blakelock's representations of nature often teeter at the cusp of expressive abstraction, evoking inner vision rather than direct observation. Blakelock's contemporaries were aware of these aspects of his art, although they often reduced his vision to the oppositional, stating what he was not rather than identifying nuances in his approach that made his art unique.

The early reviewers of Blakelock's mature aesthetic considered his work in language that suited the artist's own stated goals, insofar as they are recorded. Four themes emerge with regularity: dreams, color, music, and mysticism.[46] The latter three have been addressed, but the first bears further study. To put our appreciation of Blakelock in context, a useful starting point is the artist's now-best-known subject matter, the Indian encampment. His twilight and nocturnal views of distantly

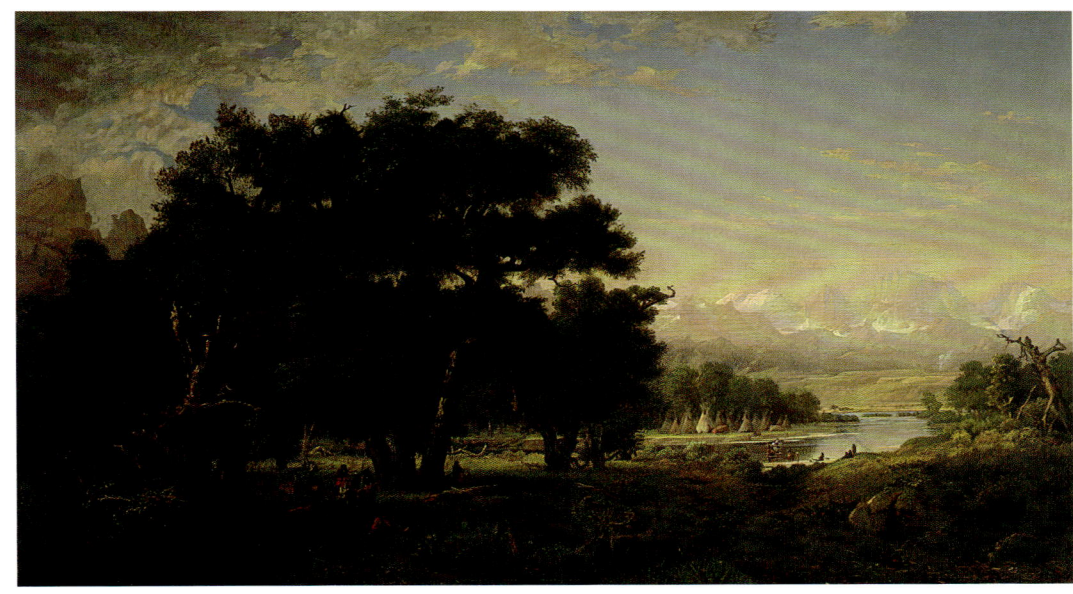

Fig. 6. Ralph Albert Blakelock, *Indian Encampment along the Snake River*, 1871, oil on canvas, 47 × 84 in., Anschutz Collection, Denver, Colorado (NBI-774).

remembered encampments offer a vestige of his early days as a realist and at the same time suggest the realm of dreams. By endowing a time-honored theme in American art with a surreal aspect, these works bridged several frontiers in the American imagination of Blakelock's day and offered a familiar, reassuring element within his otherwise unconventional art.

Significantly, as Blakelock reached the peak of his career, the frontier era in American history approached its conclusion. In 1890, the superintendent of the Census announced the end of the frontier, as settled and unsettled areas were no longer separated by a single threshold. Three years later, in an epoch-making address at the World's Columbian Exposition in Chicago, historian Frederick Jackson Turner described the significance of the event, "the closing of a great historic movement. Up to our own day American history has been in a large degree the history of the colonization of the Great West. The existence of an area of free land, its continuous recession, and the advance of American settlement westward, explain American development."[47] As the reality of the West passed into national memory, so too did Blakelock's own experience from his travels. The frontier had embedded itself in the American imagination, however, and its closure only amplified its position in the nation's collective unconscious. In their reviews, critics placed Blakelock's western landscapes in the realm of memory, precisely where the frontier itself lingered in American minds.[48]

Having experienced the frontier personally, Blakelock modeled his early masterpiece, *Indian Encampment along the Snake River* (fig. 6) squarely within the tradition of western landscape painting exemplified by Albert Bierstadt, Thomas Moran, and Worthington Whittredge (1820–1910). Completed shortly after his return to New York, *Indian Encampment along the Snake River* shares with the works of Bierstadt and his contemporaries the direct observation from nature as well as a commitment to the prevailing conventions of the picturesque on a large scale. The work demonstrates Blakelock's mastery of naturalistic detail and color, narrative composition, spatial recession, and atmospheric effects. Only the shadowy foreground offers any glimpse of the artist's later direction. As *Indian Encampment along the Snake River* demonstrates, Blakelock, who is often characterized as a self-taught artist as a means of explaining the reductiveness of his later aesthetic, was an exceptional technician who steered a different aesthetic course from the mainstream. Appropriately, *Indian Encampment along the Snake River* is also a daylight scene, reflecting its objectivity and attention to detail, both aspects that would ebb in Blakelock's later penumbral and nocturnal encampments. As Walt Whitman observed of the plains, "I was thinking the day most splendid till I saw what the not-day exhibited. . . . Now while the great thoughts of space and eternity fill me I will measure myself by them."[49]

The encampments define Blakelock's legacy, and they are his leading, although not only, contributions to American art. Used interchangeably, two are consistently held up as the exemplars of Blakelock's art, *Moonlight, Indian Encampment* (fig. 7) and *Moonlight* (Brooklyn Museum). Although both works invest an idealized rendering of the West with the mystery of night, *Moonlight, Indian Encampment* is infused with a haunting, limpid blue in the distant landscape that is unmistakably redolent of the color choices for which the artist was most admired in his day. The work embodies the identifiable traits

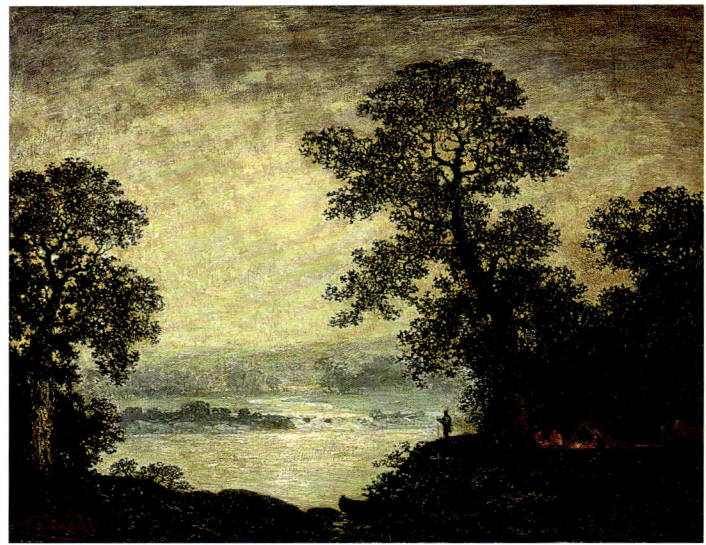

Fig. 7. RALPH ALBERT BLAKELOCK, *Moonlight, Indian Encampment*, about 1885–89, oil on canvas, 27⅛ × 34⅛ in., Smithsonian American Art Museum, Washington, DC, Gift of John Gellatly (NBI-85).

of Blakelock's mature work, including the majestic trees silhouetted by twilight or moonlight, a solitary figure contemplating the passage of night, and the serenity of a body of water in the middleground that reflects the light and tone of evening. Both works are less than three feet wide, certainly substantial but far less impressive than his monumental *Indian Encampment along the Snake River*. What may have been his most ambitious later work, the Metropolitan Museum of Art's *Indian Encampment*, was reportedly reduced in size at the suggestion of Blakelock's friend and patron Harry Watrous.[51] Were it doubled in size, the painting would indeed have been larger than *Snake River*. *Brook by Moonlight* is a rare instance of a large-scale composition from

Blakelock's mature period. For the most part, however, his later works are smaller, and truly intimate, reflecting the artist's inward turn.

Among the keys to appreciating Blakelock's interiority is his contemplative *At Nature's Mirror* (plate 14). A female nude sits beside a small pond and looks down toward her reflection in the water. The subject is an adaptation of the ancient tale of Narcissus, who drowned while obsessing over his reflection in a similar body of water, paralleling the self-reflective nature of Blakelock's own art. Similar to the figure in his earlier *Captive*, the nude is almost entirely devoid of erotism. Instead, she has folded her legs, joined her hands, and bowed her head in a gesture of introversion and closure. Absorbed in her experience of nature, the figure's nudity appears itself symbolic, a reminder of her vulnerability. Here, deep in nature, the figure returns to her most fundamental concerns, stripped of the trappings of society. The imposing boulder across the pond completes the figure's isolation, enclosing her rather than opening the view outward to a broader expanse of space. The landscape around the figure exemplifies Blakelock's introversion, even as the figure in the foreground is absorbed in her self-reflection.

How could Blakelock's style have transformed so dramatically within the depiction of his western landscapes without an attendant change in subject matter? Perhaps because the subject matter itself had varying associations for the artist. John Wilmerding has recently explored the subject of American artists' signatures and how they can suggest the degree of an artist's personal investment in a particular work.[51] Wilmerding devotes particular attention to the varied practices of Winslow Homer (1836–1910), but Blakelock too exercised an unusual method of signing his name, consistently enclosing it in the shape of an arrowhead. The arrowhead is not only the weapon's lethal tip, it is also its most enduring fragment, a vestige of ancient civilizations. From this perspective, Blakelock's visions of Indian encampments by night not only reflect the impending extinction of Native American culture in the modern period but also the prehistoric cultures that had come before contact with Western civilizations. Even at its least symbolic, Blakelock's arrowhead conveys a sense of the artist's personal investment in his art and his identification with Native American subjects. When Blakelock first rendered his western scenes, they were documents of his experience and observations, but with time they became documents of his memory, as well as the memory of the nation at large.

At his most original, Blakelock found landscapes and encampments all around him, including among the pigments on his palette, on the rough finish of his bathtub, and, of course, lurking in accumulated layers on his canvases. He worked and reworked his compositions until a scene emerged. This was not painting by observation but painting by insight. The tantalizing title of Blakelock's single known treatise on art, of which only the title page remains, is "Measure and Weight: On the Art of Painting."[52] We can only speculate as to the essay's content, but his practice of building up and then scraping down, only to rebuild once more, suggests a constant process of moving, balancing, and weighing forms and colors within his compositions on a purely abstract level before entering the realm of figuration. We can imagine the final elements of Blakelock's compositions suggesting themselves in the amorphous specters that appeared by accident rather than by design. The artist's practice balanced creation with erasure, the outcome gradually coalescing into forms that Blakelock's conscious mind could perceive in the intuitive work of his hand or in the world around him. The artist's wife recalled Blakelock's unusual practice, telling "of his habit of seeing pictures, compositions in everything,— the markings on old boards; the broken or worn enamel in the bathtub being a field of great suggestiveness."[53] In this phase of his art, Blakelock could hardly have been further from earlier realist practice.

With this degree of personal expression, Blakelock's frequent choice of Native American subjects and his arrowhead-enclosed signature resound with greater significance, linking his western and unconscious frontiers. Blakelock's art reinforced the common conception of Native American civilizations as primitive and attuned to nature in a way that Euro-Americans were not. By enmeshing his intuitive aesthetic with Native American subjects, Blakelock anticipated European modernist aesthetics of the early twentieth century, as well as the forays into the subconscious practiced later by the surrealists. To his contemporaries, however, Blakelock's art exceeded expectations about what art was or could be, which critic Kirk Henry referred to as "wild adventures into the realm of tonality."[54] He shared so little with prevailing taste, particularly in abandoning the tenets of realism, that critics had to take a position, and they either consigned him to the ranks of the incompetent or embraced his novelty as a sign of things to come. Few remained on the sidelines.

The deep, meditative tenor of Blakelock's compositions resonates with a fatalistic strain of later nineteenth-century American society following the Civil War. As art historian Sarah Burns has observed in a recent study, the gothic mode, to which much of Blakelock's art adheres, provided artists with "a potent, fluid language for dealing with darker facets of history and the psyche that seldom intruded into the optimistic domains of more conventional landscape and genre painting."[55] Although Blakelock makes virtually no appearance in Burns's study except as a foil for the more fortunate path of Albert Pinkham Ryder, his art resonates with her thesis.[56] In particular, Blakelock's choice of Native Americans as the intermediaries of his visionary landscapes grounds his art in American experience. The figure of the Native American had been associated with the primeval American landscape since long before the romantic visions of Thomas Cole found favor during the 1820s. As Native American society appeared to approach extinction and the idea of the frontier became obsolete, Blakelock's scenes suggested a twilight of American culture itself, as its deepest archetype, the Native American, threatened to disappear.

CONCLUSION

How are we to reconcile the historical Blakelock with the mad genius that has dominated scholarship since the turn of the century? He never achieved the recognition or affluence enjoyed by several of his peers, and yet he received a substantial amount of attention in the press and from collectors. Loyal friends helped him during difficult times, and his wife remained utterly devoted to their family despite their financial struggles and his disability. This is hardly the story of a madman. Blakelock believed in his art and was convinced of his own originality and contribution. By setting aside, even briefly, the artist's later condition, we gain a rich new appreciation of his art, as Blakelock himself asked.

Before his institutionalization, critics juggled Blakelock within their standard practice of charting artists relative to one another and to a commonly accepted register of past masters.

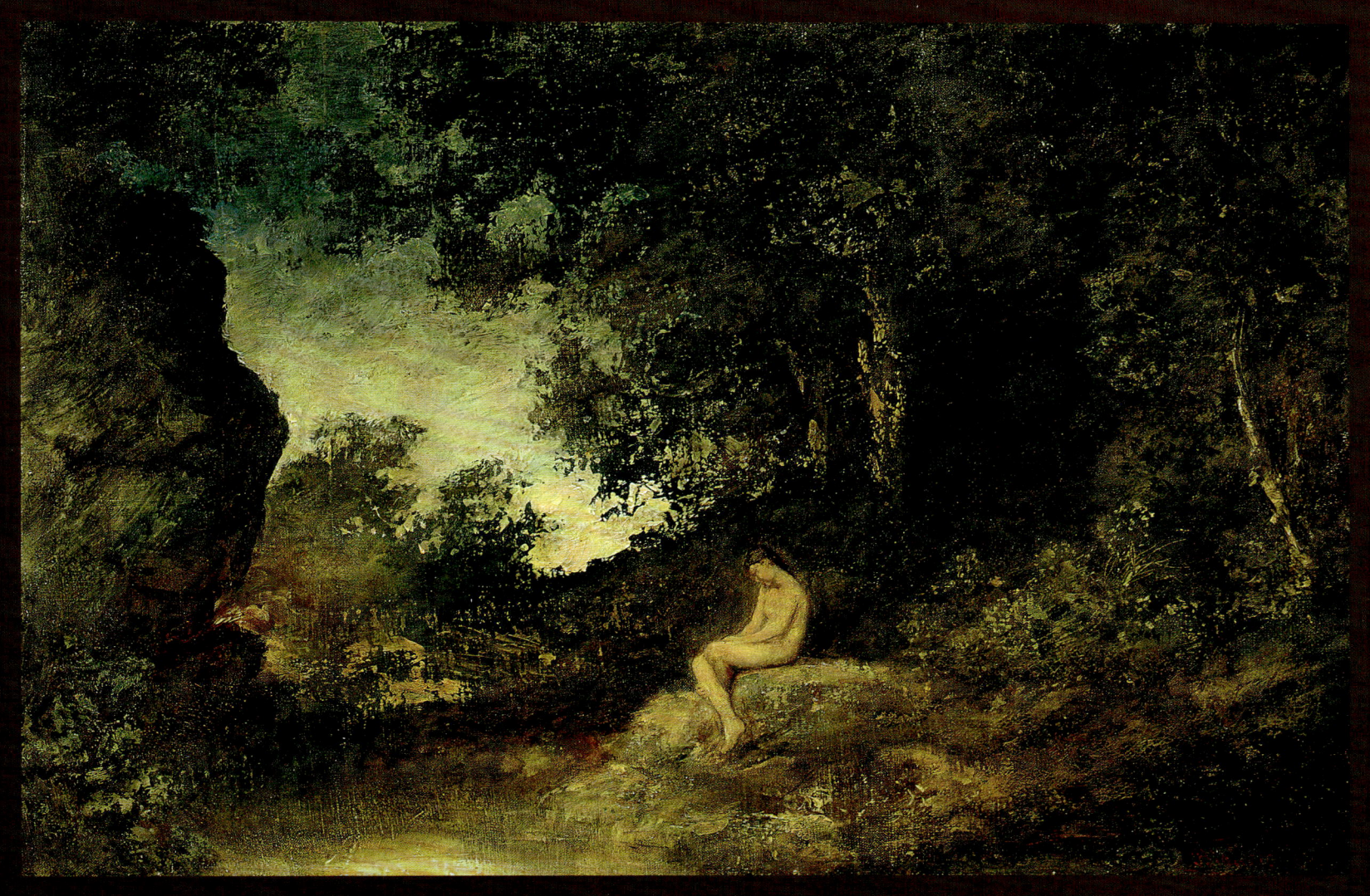

14 *At Nature's Mirror, about 1880*

In order to make sense of this radical painter, they struggled to reassess their fundamental belief that good art was descriptive. Blakelock, joined in the collective mind with Ryder, opened the door to an abstract, expressive system of colorism. As characterized by critics and early biographers, Blakelock's art set the stage for modernism in America during the early twentieth century, particularly in its turn to Indian cultures and the western landscape to formulate an intrinsically American vision. The lesson of studying Blakelock's art through the eyes of his contemporaries is that his mature aesthetic looked forward to modernism rather than back to the Hudson River School or to western documentary painting. He was truly a visionary in all senses.

NOTES

1. Lewis W. Francis recalled Blakelock's remark in a letter to art historian Lloyd Goodrich (26 February 1947). Son of the pastor of Greenpoint Reformed Church in Brooklyn, Francis had attended Blakelock's wedding to Cora Rebecca Bailey in 1877 (according to Mrs. Blakelock, it was 1875, but her recollection of dates has proven unreliable as she herself confessed) and remembered the artist's reply to concern over his apparent lack of income, which induced him to pay the pastor's fee with a painting in lieu of cash. Francis's letter is held in the extensive Blakelock Archives at the Frick Art Reference Library in New York. The Blakelock Archives document the research conducted by Goodrich and his assistant Rosalind Irvine in preparation for the artist's 1947 retrospective at the Whitney Museum of American Art.

2. Sadakichi Hartmann, *A History of American Art* (Boston: L. C. Page, 1901), 1:108.

3. Elliott Daingerfield, *Ralph Albert Blakelock* (New York: Frederic Fairchild Sherman, 1914), 8. Anonymous, "Trying to Call Blakelock," *New York Times Magazine* (April 2, 1916), 7.

4. In his recent biography of Blakelock, Glyn Vincent observes that the artist's father was a police officer before turning to medicine by 1861. Vincent's discussion of the artist's possible poverty during this period supports the author's own version of the artist's rags-to-riches "Horatio Alger" story but is primarily circumstantial. Glyn Vincent, *The Unknown Night: The Genius and Madness of R. A. Blakelock, An American Painter* (New York: Grove Press, 2003), 36–37, 42–44, 312–13.

5. Mrs. Ralph Albert Blakelock to Robert C. Vose, 10 January 1906, private collection; copy at the Nebraska Blakelock Inventory, University of Nebraska–Lincoln.

6. Abraham Davidson has speculated that Blakelock might have made two trips west, the first in 1869 and the second in 1871, based on dated drawings. Abraham A. Davidson, *Ralph Albert Blakelock* (University Park, PA: The Pennsylvania State University Press, 1996), 15–16.

7. Daingerfield, 12.

8. Cited in Vincent, 145.

9. Gustav Kobbe, "Belated Honors Come to Ralph Blakelock, Painter, 16 Years Insane," *New York Herald* (May 4, 1913), magazine section, 2.

10. Daingerfield, 19.

11. Mrs. Ralph Albert Blakelock to Robert C. Vose, 26 February 1908, private collection; copy at the Nebraska Blakelock Inventory.

12. Lloyd Goodrich, *Ralph Albert Blakelock Centennial Exhibition* (New York: Whitney Museum of American Art, 1947), 23.

13. Anonymous, "American Paintings and Impressionist Paintings in New York Galleries," *Boston Evening Transcript* (July 20, 1893), 4.

14. Frederick W. Morton, "Work of Ralph Albert Blakelock," *Brush and Pencil* 9, no. 5 (February 1902), 263–64.

15. Ibid., 257.

16. Goodrich, 14.

17. Ibid.

18. Anonymous, "Ralph Albert Blakelock," *The Collector* 2, no. 4 (December 15, 1890), 43.

19. Annette Blaugrund, *The Tenth Street Studio Building: Artist-Entrepreneurs from the Hudson River School to the American Impressionists* (Southampton, NY: The Parrish Art Museum, 1997), 133.

20. Abraham A. Davidson, "Art and Insanity, One Case," *Smithsonian Studies in American Art* 3, no. 3 (Summer 1989), 57.

21. Daingerfield, 19.

22. See Davidson, "Art and Insanity," and Dorinda Evans, "Art and Deception: Ralph Blakelock and his Guardian," *American Art Journal* 19, no. 1 (Winter 1987), 39–50.

23. Inness wrote about his art, whereas Blakelock was mute. The analogy of colors to language in Inness's work comes from an 1881 review in the *Boston Independent*. Cited in Nicolai Cikovsky Jr., "George Inness and Tonalist Uncertainty," in Ralph Sessions, et al, *The Poetic Vision: American Tonalism* (Exh. cat., New York: Spanierman Gallery, 2005), 52.

24. Cited in biographical entry for *Appleton's Cyclopedia of American Biography* (New York: Appleton & Co., 1887), 1:287.

25. Anonymous, "Some Paintings by Ralph Albert Blakelock," *The Artist* 29 (January 1901), 18.

26. Anonymous, "Blakelock and his Genius," *Suburban Society* 1, no. 10 (April 28, 1916), 3–4.

27. John Wilmerding, *American Art* (New York: Penguin Books, 1976), 165.

28. Cited in "Blakelock, Free for Day, Sees His Pictures Here," *New York Tribune* (April 12, 1916), 9.

29. Cited in Goodrich, 20.

30. Daingerfield speculated that Blakelock's *Pegasus* was not a finished work and might eventually have become an Indian hunter. Daingerfield, 23.

31. Elizabeth Broun has suggested that Ryder's proximate source for the *Flying Dutchmen* might have been Captain Frederick Marryat's 1839 novel *The Phantom Ship.* Given that Ryder's several other works derived from Wagner, however, that source remains likely. Broun, *Albert Pinkham Ryder* (Washington and London: Smithsonian Institution Press, 1990), 222.

32. Davidson, *Ralph Albert Blakelock,* 67.

33. Cited in Judith Zilczer, "'Color Music': Synaesthesia and Nineteenth-Century Sources for Abstract Art," *Artibus et Historiae* 8, no. 16 (1987), 101.

34. Charles Caffin, *The Story of American Painting: The Evolution of Painting in America from Colonial Times to the Present* (New York: Frederick A. Stokes, 1907), 217.

35. Morton, 260.

36. James William Pattison, "The Art of Blakelock," *Fine Arts Journal* 27, no. 4 (October 1912), 646.

37. Daingerfield, 28.

38. N. N. [Elizabeth Pennell],"Blakelock," *The Nation* (August 23, 1919), 255.

39. Aaron Sheon, *Monticelli: His Contemporaries, His Influence* (Pittsburgh, PA: Museum of Art, Carnegie Institute, 1978), 9.

40. Ibid., 87, 109 n32.

41. The most productive study to date is found in Davidson, *Ralph Albert Blakelock,* 130–34. Most studies make at least passing reference to his Swedenborgianism, which is documented in the later recollections of family members, but few explore it or its significance to his work.

42. Inness, reprinted in Sally Promey, "The Ribband of Faith: George Inness, Color Theory, and the Swedenborgian Church," *American Art Journal* 26, no. 1/2 (1994), 46.

43. Ibid., 58.

44. *Appleton's,* 1:287.

45. Eugene Taylor, "The Interior Landscape: George Inness and William James on Art from a Swedenborgian Point of View," *Archives of American Art Journal* 37, no. 1/2 (1997), 2.

46. The primary critique of Blakelock's art at the time was that it lacked naturalism, which was hardly criticism at all given that the artist's work so clearly and deliberately broke with the American tradition of detailed realism.

47. Reprinted in Frederick Jackson Turner, *Rereading Frederick Jackson Turner: "The Significance of the Frontier in American History," and Other Essays* (New Haven and London: Yale University Press, 1998), 31.

48. Blakelock's imagined western scenes certainly came to national prominence during the period of his confinement, but that period also coincided with a wave of nostalgia for the bygone era of the western frontier.

49. Walt Whitman, "Night on the Prairies" (1860), reprinted in *Leaves of Grass* (New York: Vintage Books/Library of America, 1992), 566.

50. Doreen Bolger Burke, *American Paintings in the Metropolitan Museum of Art, Volume III, A Catalogue of Works by Artists Born between 1846 and 1864* (New York: Metropolitan Museum of Art, in association with Princeton University Press, 1980), 40–41.

51. John Wilmerding, *Signs of the Artist: Signatures and Self-Expression in American Paintings* (New Haven and London: Yale University Press, 2003).

52. Vincent, 186.

53. Daingerfield, 16.

54. Kirk D. Henry, "An American Patron of American Art," *Brush and Pencil* 8 (July 1901), 220–21.

55. Sarah Burns, *Painting the Dark Side: Art and the Gothic Imagination in Nineteenth-Century America* (Berkeley: University of California Press, 2004), xx.

56. Ibid., 244.

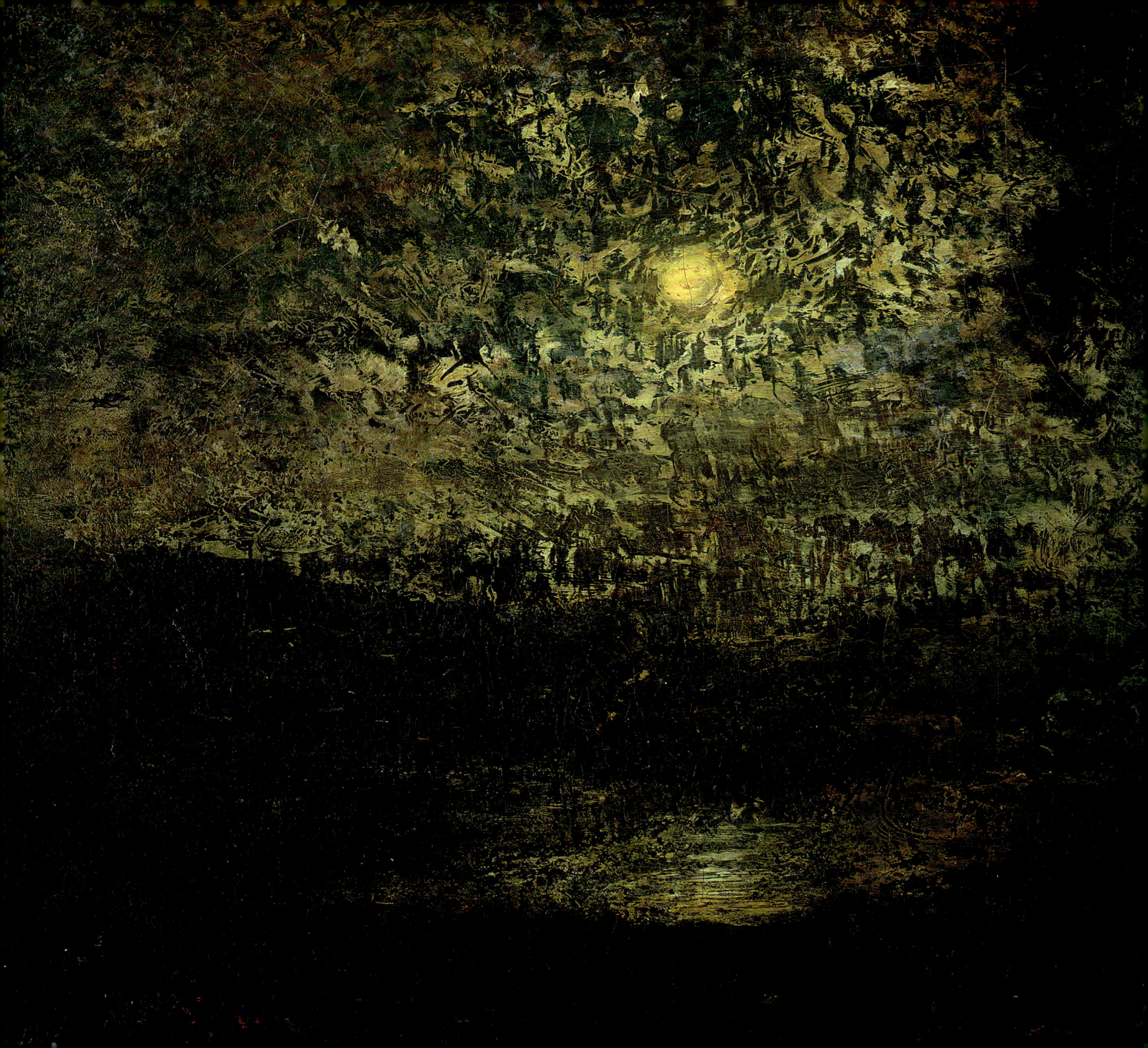

R. A. Blakelock and Contemporary Painting: Curatorial Reflections

DANIEL A. SIEDELL

For Norman

ome painters, including myself, do not care what chair they are sitting on. It does not even have to be a comfortable one. They are too nervous to find out where they ought to sit. They do not want to "sit in style." Rather, they have found that painting—any kind of painting, any style of painting—to be painting at all, in fact—is a way of living today, a style of living so to speak. That is where the form of it lies.

WILLEM DE KOONING, "What Abstract Art Means to Me," 1951[1]

I

Art history is ambivalent toward Ralph Albert Blakelock. He is usually mentioned behind Albert Pinkham Ryder (1847–1917) as one of the important visionary landscape painters of the later nineteenth century. Scholars observe that Blakelock lacked Ryder's education and imagination and that his career, although punctuated with some success, was marred by mental illness, which thus limited his artistic development. There are many reasons for this ambivalent assessment, some obvious, others less so. Blakelock's mental illness seems to overpower his paintings. It is this sensational aspect of his life that seems to receive attention. When his paintings like the moonlights and Indian encampments are discussed, they tend to be described as little more than visual illustrations of the artist's tragic life. In reference to the Smithsonian American Art Museum's *Moonlight, Indian Encampment* (1885–89), Wayne Craven suggests, "The trees, silhouetted against a luminous sky, are built up in a thick impasto, and there is a nervousness in their forms that suggests the mental problems the artist was to experience."[2] That in 1913 one of Blakelock's moonlight paintings commanded the highest price ever paid for a work by a living American artist has not improved his reputation among critics and scholars. Rather, it seems only to have reinforced the historical vagaries and vicissitudes of taste and fashion.

Blakelock's surge in popularity, which occurred only after he had been institutionalized in 1891, was located in his easily recognizable moonlight and Indian encampment scenes. His popularity tended to limit the scope of Blakelock's artistic production, which, combined with his sudden rise in recognition, generated a cottage industry of fake Blakelock paintings. These factors reduced Blakelock to a one-trick pony, the significance of whose work is compromised because it was too easily copied. But the fakes, forgeries, and copies were made by those who did not understand the formal complexities of Blakelock's practice, reducing his work to content, to imagery, which has, over time, obscured Blakelock's aesthetic achievement.

Among the less obvious reasons for Blakelock's visible absence in the art historical literature is the scant textual evidence that art historians can lean on. Almost nothing survives of Blakelock's views on his painting and art in general. He was self-taught and therefore not a product of the traditional mentor-disciple model of artistic development. He also did not have any students or disciples himself. Art historians are, by and large, a text-based lot. They need archives, written correspondence, and other materials to establish historical value and determine achievement. With Blakelock, once we leave the tragic and sordid realm of his mental life, we are left only with the paintings. This is hardly the foundation on which art historians are comfortable building an art-historical presence.

When Blakelock did receive some critical and commercial success and attention, he had already been confined to a mental institution. That art historians often compare Blakelock unfavorably to Ryder has also to do with the latter's more

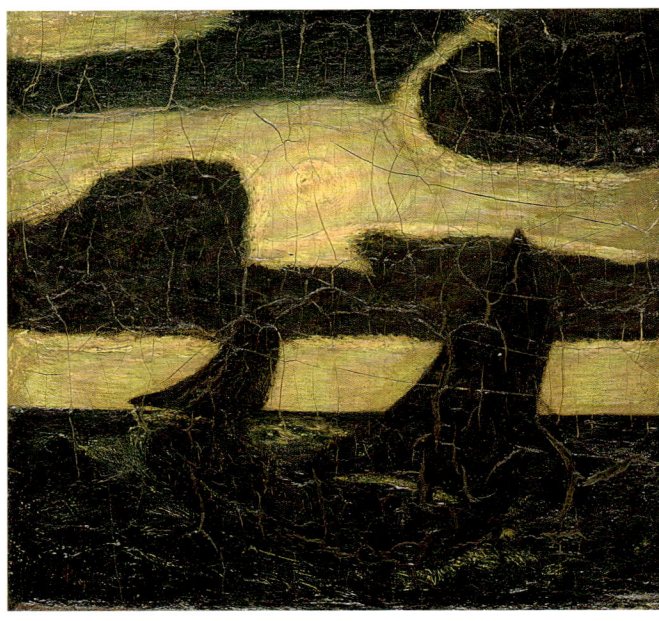

Fig. 1. ALBERT PINKHAM RYDER (1847–1917), *Moonlight Marine*, 1870–90, oil and possibly wood on wax panel, 11½ × 12 in., The Metropolitan Museum of Art, Samuel D. Lee Fund, 1934 (34.55). Photograph © The Metropolitan Museum of Art, New York.

literary paintings, which are interpreted within and through Ryder's more robust intellectual development and interests and give the appearance of being more profound and deeper than Blakelock's because they rely on an iconography derived from literature and culture (fig. 1).

Second, art history is written from the vantage point of the present, and the present, like the past, has adversely affected Blakelock's achievement. The development of American art history as a discrete scholarly field emerged in the late 1940s and

1950s as an outgrowth of the work of critics and curators eager to develop American precedents for abstract expressionism. The result was an intense reevaluation of nineteenth-century American landscape paintings that, while establishing abstract expressionism's American roots, also led to a revival of interest in the painters of the Hudson River School, the tonalists, the luminists, and the so-called visionaries, especially Ryder, who enjoyed a major retrospective, curated by Lloyd Goodrich, at the Whitney Museum of American Art in 1947. Art historians still consider Ryder to be an important influence on abstract expressionism, and perhaps a not insignificant reason is the fact that ten of Ryder's paintings were included in the Armory Show of 1913, an inclusion that firmly embedded Ryder in modernist discourse a generation earlier, a discourse on which Ryder's 1947 Whitney retrospective merely built. Blakelock, however, was not included in the Armory Show, much to the consternation and objections of several important American modernist painters, among them Marsden Hartley, who was also instrumental in championing Ryder's significance.[3]

Despite the fact that Blakelock's work did not enjoy the early modernist interpretative framework afforded by the Armory Show, it was rediscovered and reevaluated at the same time as Ryder's. Lloyd Goodrich also organized a retrospective of Blakelock's work for the Whitney in 1947. Goodrich tried to argue for the contemporary relevance of Blakelock's work as it related to the new American painting that was emerging on the New York art scene. He observed:

But Blakelock was more than a simple recorder of nature's appearances. He was always highly conscious of pattern. The delicate tracery of foliage against the sky

had to be not only convincing as representation but fine as decoration. He used twilight and moonlight to create a unified tone, to simplify forms, to drop veils between foreground and distance, to create recession.[4]

Goodrich attempted to draw attention away from Blakelock's content to his form, his pattern, his interest in the abstract aspects of painting. In an effort to bind Blakelock to the very heart of abstraction through Wassily Kandinsky and the synchromists Morgan Russell and Stanton Macdonald-Wright, Goodrich wrote, "Often his color is conceived in a musical sense, with little relation to naturalist truth."[5] And finally, "He had a strongly sensuous feeling for texture and surface, for the purely physical properties of pigment and material."[6] And it is this sense of "texture and surface," which was becoming evident in the work of de Kooning and Jackson Pollock, that Goodrich was keen to point out in Blakelock.

Goodrich also draws attention away from Blakelock's content and to his form to interpret his limited range of subjects as variations on a theme in which he explores formal innovation. Color, texture, harmony, and pattern, rather than diversity of subject matter, was intended to put the artist's work into the framework that was beginning to brew at Peggy Guggenheim's Art of This Century Gallery, with Pollock, Robert Motherwell, Mark Rothko, and others. The art critic Robert Coates observed, "Blakelock was completely outside his period artistically, and despite his early attempts to conform he could not help moving further and further away from the accepted tradition as his style matured."[7]

The 1947 Whitney retrospective and Goodrich's efforts to demonstrate Blakelock's aesthetic prescience was no doubt the

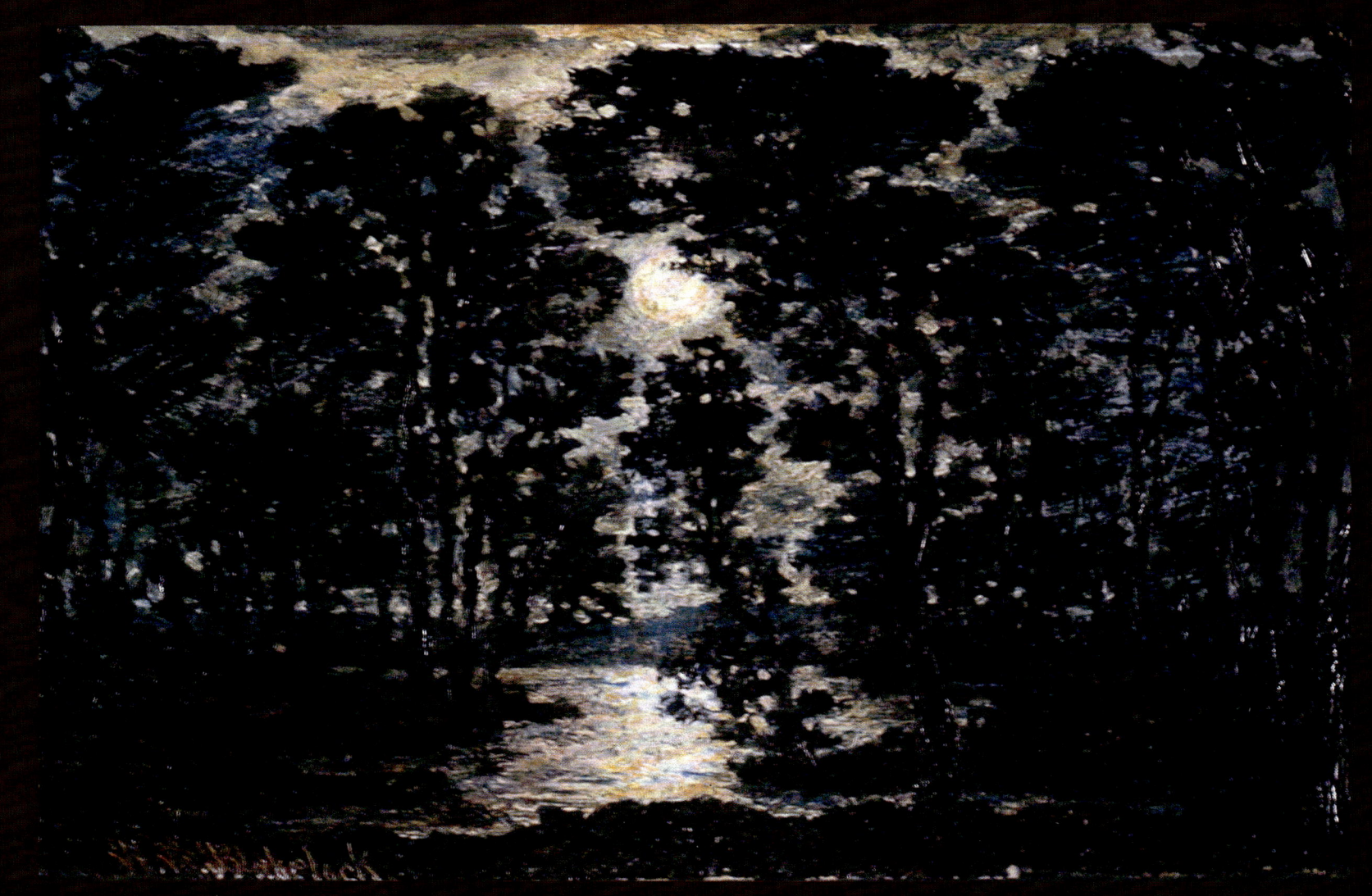

15 *Heavy Woods—Moonlight*, undated

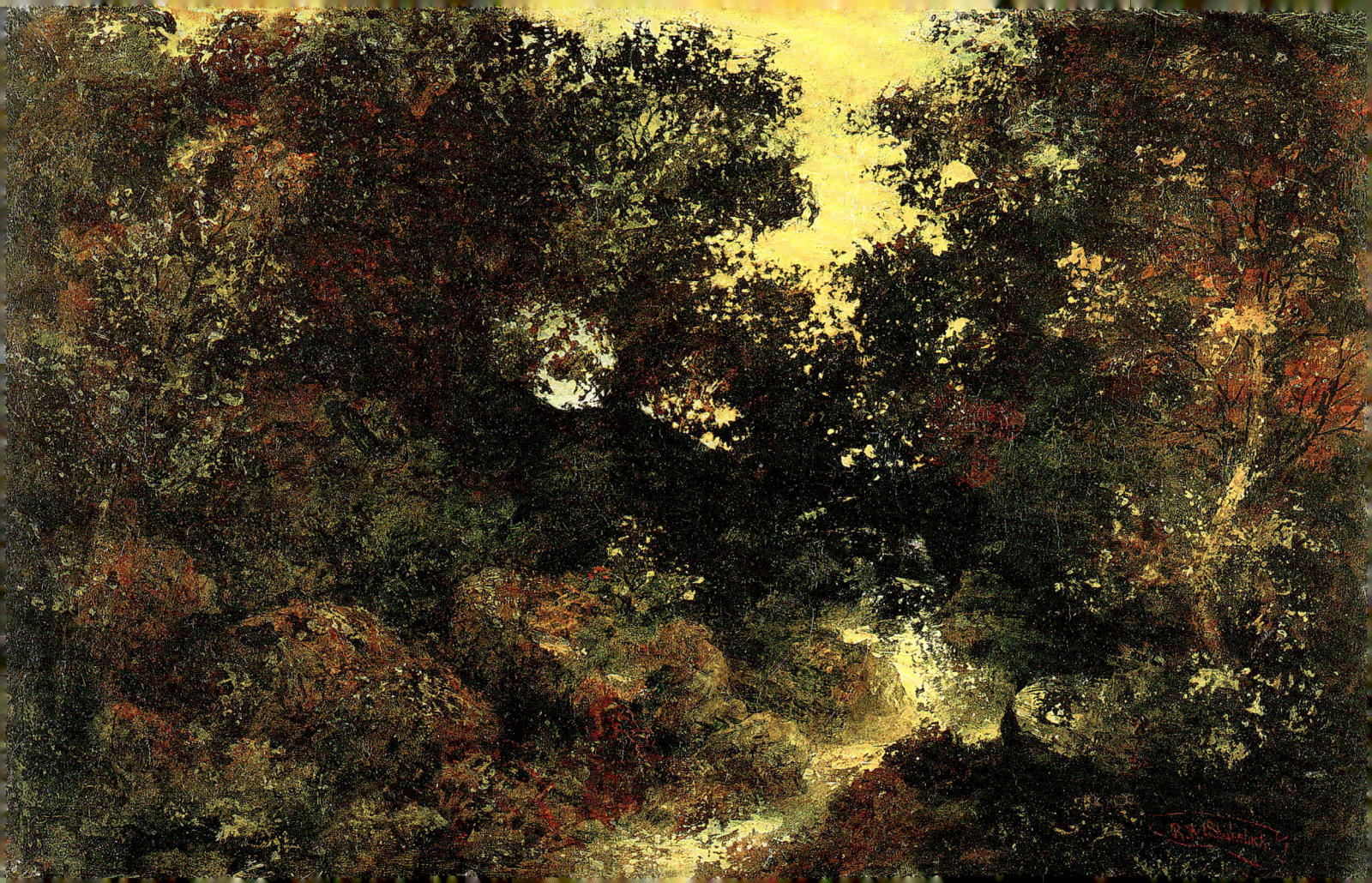

reason behind William Seitz's mention of Blakelock's intense subjectivity, albeit in the context of an appreciation of Ryder, in his 1955 doctoral dissertation on abstract expressionism, the first book-length study on the movement.[8] Seitz writes:

> Not only was Ryder more pointedly subjective than any American romantic save John Quidor . . . and Ralph Blakelock, and not only did he manipulate pigment for itself, he was by all odds the most abstract American painter of the late nineteenth century. He shaped and reshaped relational flat areas on a heavily painted and repainted surface. The fundamental elements of Abstract Expressionism are all implicit: picture plane, active and personal use of the medium for itself, unfinish, relational uses of flat shapes, and abstract naturalism.[9]

Seitz continues, "It is no wonder that Hans Hofmann and Jackson Pollock find Ryder the only nineteenth-century American artist with whom they feel kinship."[10] (There is, however, an abstract expressionist painter whose kinship leans toward Blakelock, an artist I will discuss below and whose work has occupied much of my art-historical research as a specialist in abstract expressionism and the New York School.)

The tissue that bound Blakelock to Ryder from the beginning of their public careers, first in derision and later in admiration, began to weaken and then tear completely as Ryder became more strongly and substantially associated with advanced twentieth-century modernist painting, especially as it served as a precedent and influence for abstract expressionism. Blakelock, however, through scholarly neglect fed by a damaged and diluted market for his work through forgeries, inferior imitations, and a flood of the artist's own hastily done pictures,

began to fade. Any kind of revival of interest in Blakelock's work that Goodrich and the Whitney generated did not last.

The connection between Blakelock and Ryder, however, is an important one. Norman A. Geske is surely correct to observe that

> Blakelock and Ryder are remarkably alike and significantly different, and their simultaneous presence within the same decades of time is perhaps a worthy subject of speculation as regards their role in the transition of American artistic effort from the nineteenth to the twentieth century. It is perhaps enough to note at this point that, while there is no propriety in seeking to devalue Ryder, there is perhaps some need to reevaluate Blakelock.[11]

This essay takes Geske's observation seriously and suggests that the complexity of Blakelock's paintings was not lost on a number of twentieth-century modernist painters who were rethinking the relationship between form and content. And although it was surely Ryder who exerted a greater influence over the majority of twentieth-century painters in the United States, this essay will attempt to open some critical space to consider Blakelock's work not in the light of a modernist precedence, but in the contemporary postmodernist context for painting.

In addition to Norman Geske's tireless efforts, Abraham Davidson has authored the only monograph on Blakelock, and the artist's biography, written by Glyn Vincent, has only recently been published. In a review of Vincent's biography, Arthur Danto observed, after looking at the Metropolitan Museum of Art's painting by Blakelock, that it "must have seemed beautiful at one time, but now it is faded and even shabby, and I was not surprised that there was nothing else by him, if it was representative." And although Danto finds some of the New York shanties pictures and Indian encampments interesting, he suggests, "It is just the masterpieces [Moonlight paintings] that have gone dry."[12] It appears evident that Danto has seen few, if any, paintings by Blakelock and before reading the biography knew very little about the artist himself.

II

My experience of Blakelock's work has been quite different, and it is through my curatorial experience that I will explore Blakelock's relevance for contemporary painting. While curator of the Sheldon Memorial Art Gallery, I have for the past ten years lived and worked with Blakelock. The Sheldon owns over thirty Blakelock paintings, and the University of Nebraska is home to the Nebraska Blakelock Inventory, initiated by Norman Geske, director emeritus of the Sheldon and pre-eminent Blakelock scholar, who continues to live and work within a short walk from both the Sheldon's collections and the inventory. I have made it a habit to include several Blakelock paintings in my permanent collection reinstallations over the years. As a result, I have developed an abiding affection for his work. I often hang his pictures next to a painting by Ryder (fig. 2); a suite of eight paintings by Arthur B. Davies, called, perhaps not coincidentally, *Moonlight Sonata* (fig. 3); and a farmhouse painting by fellow Swedenborgian enthusiast George Inness (fig. 4). Not only do the Blakelock paintings I regularly exhibit stand up aesthetically to these other paintings, but I have noticed that, following Goodrich, they seem even to fit well with our collection of early twentieth-century modernist

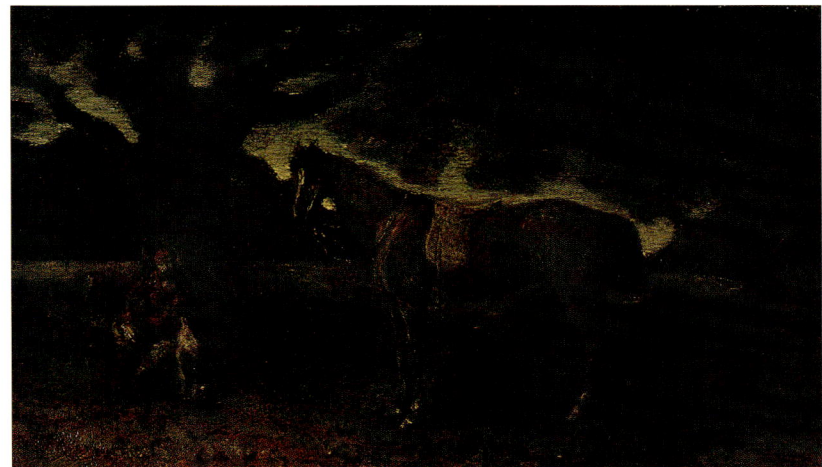

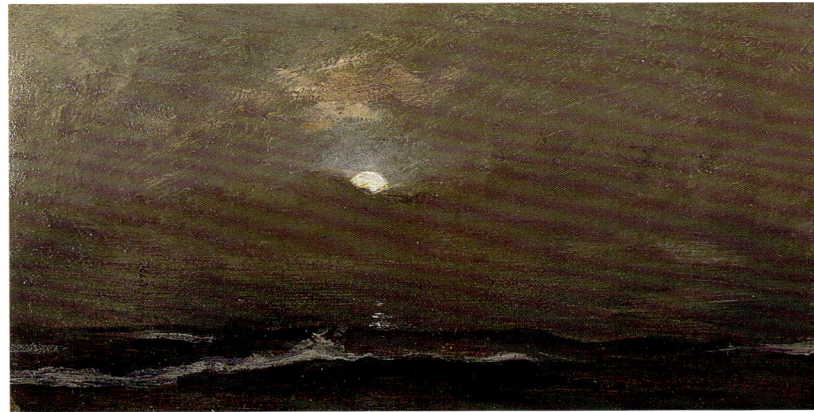

Fig. 2. ALBERT PINKHAM RYDER, *Hunter's Rest*, 1890, oil on canvas, 13¾ × 23½ in., Sheldon Memorial Art Gallery and Sculpture Garden, University of Nebraska–Lincoln, NAA—Thomas C. Woods Memorial Collection, 1961, N-134.

Fig. 3. ARTHUR BOWEN DAVIES, *Moonlight Sonata (moon, sea with pink cloud)*, about 1890, oil on board, 4½ × 8⅝ in., Sheldon Memorial Art Gallery and Sculpture Garden, University of Nebraska–Lincoln, NAA—Gift of Jo Ann Kimball in memory of Curtis Kimball Jr., 1979, N-655.

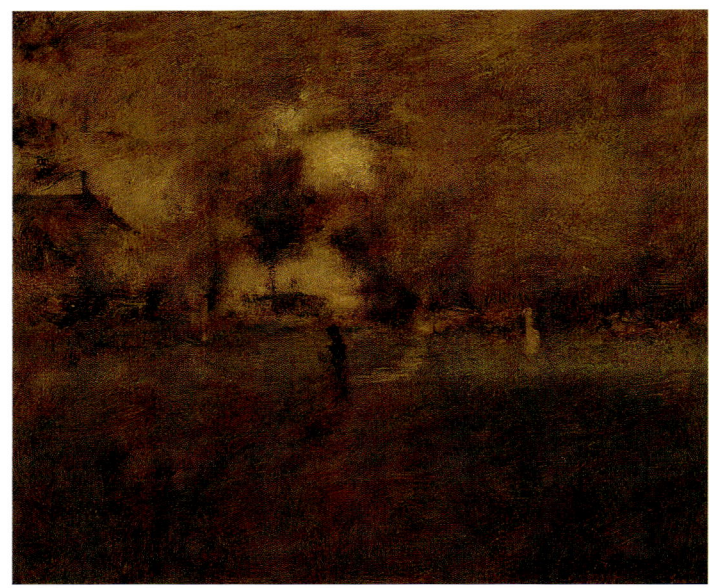

Fig. 4. GEORGE INNESS, *The Farmhouse*, about 1894, oil on canvas, 25¼ × 30¼ in., Sheldon Memorial Art Gallery and Sculpture Garden, University of Nebraska–Lincoln, NAA—Given in loving memory of Lorraine LeMar Rohman by Melanie R. Waites, Carl P. Rohman II, Stephen L. Rohman, and G. Peter D. Rohman, 1985, N-674.

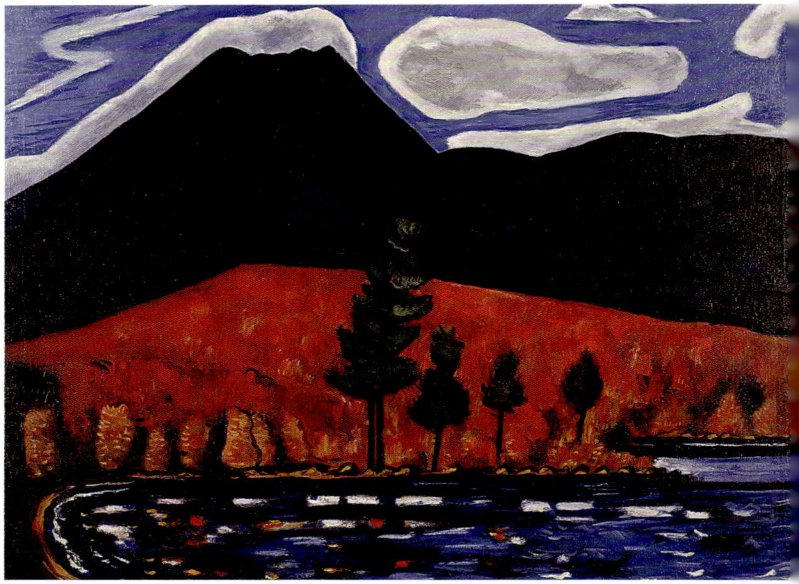

Fig. 5. MARSDEN HARTLEY, *Mount Katahdin, Autumn, No. 1*, about 1939–40, oil on canvas, 29⅜ × 39¾ in., Sheldon Memorial Art Gallery and Sculpture Garden, University of Nebraska–Lincoln, UNL—F. M. Hall Collection, 1943, H-232.

paintings, from Joseph Stella's *Battle of Lights, Coney Island* and Marsden Hartley's *Mount Katahdin, Autumn No. 1* (fig. 5) to works by Louis Eilshemius (fig. 6), John Marin, Maurice Prendergast, and even our collection of abstract expressionist paintings, especially an early painting by Clyfford Still (fig. 7). Clearly, from the curatorial perspective of the Sheldon's permanent collection, Blakelock belongs in the twentieth century. From my own curatorial perspective, shaped by the context of the Sheldon's strong permanent collections of nineteenth- and twentieth-century American art, Blakelock's paintings play a

significant role and command considerable attention. In fact, the Sheldon's *Moonlight* (plate 8) is one of the more important paintings that I use to tell the story of the development of contemporary American painting.

But my approach to Blakelock stems from my work as a curator of contemporary art, not as a scholar of nineteenth-century American painting. I present Blakelock's paintings as a result of what I understand to be their relevance for contemporary art. Blakelock's work illumes aspects of both modernist and postmodernist painting in the Sheldon's collection.

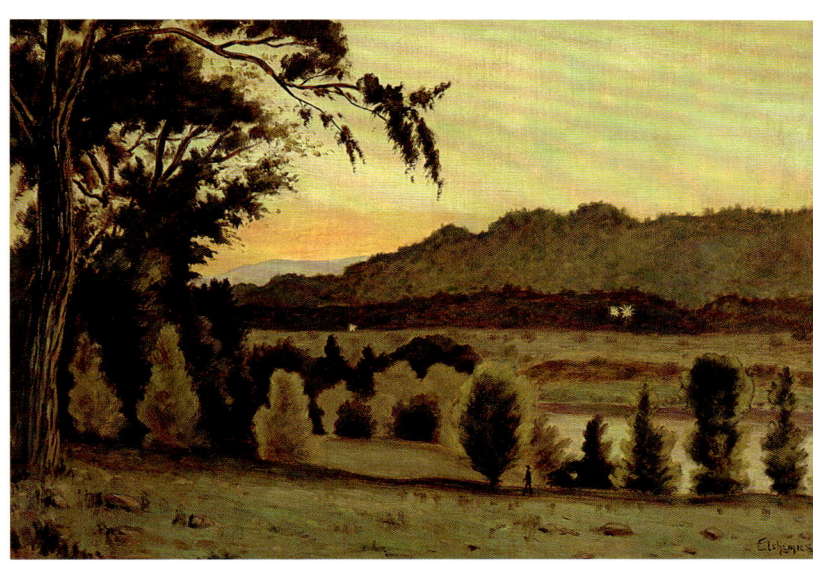

Fig. 6. Louis Michel Eilshemius, *Evening Light, Ellenville, NY*, 1901, oil on canvas, 19¾ × 29¾ in., Sheldon Memorial Art Gallery and Sculpture Garden, University of Nebraska–Lincoln, NAA—Thomas C. Woods Memorial, 1959, N-118.

This unconventional, perhaps even heterodox, perspective on Blakelock has been reinforced by a phenomenon that has occurred too often to be merely coincidental. When on public view, the Blakelock paintings receive considerable attention from practicing painters. Not only are painters working in Nebraska drawn to the Blakelock paintings, which have been part of the Sheldon's collection for forty years, visiting artists, often artists with whom I am working on projects, seem always to single them out for special attention as they linger in our permanent collection galleries.

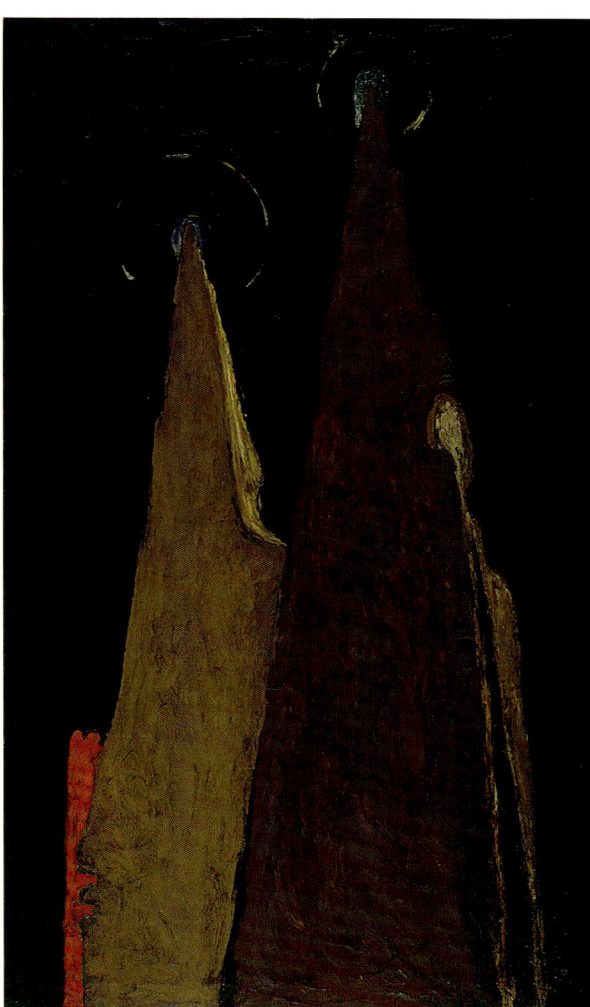

Fig. 7. Clyfford Still, *Untitled*, 1946, oil on canvas, 58¼ × 33¼ in., Sheldon Memorial Art Gallery and Sculpture Garden, University of Nebraska–Lincoln, UNL—Olga N. Sheldon Acquisition Trust, 1997, U-4959.

My curatorial approach and the responses of artists are based exclusively on formal issues. What is needed in reassessing Blakelock is to attend more closely to the paintings themselves. Again, except for Geske's analyses, little attention has been paid directly to the paintings by critics and art historians. What follows is an attempt to articulate Blakelock's significance from the vantage point of my experience with two seemingly unrelated artists, one an abstract modernist painter, another a postabstract representational painter.

III

It is often said that there are "painters' painters," those artists who, for one reason or another, receive more attention from fellow artists than from critics, curators, and art historians. There is a craft to painting that cuts through modernism, antimodernism, and postmodernism; through representation, abstraction, and nonobjectivism as well. Every painter in the Western tradition is faced with the challenge of applying pigment to a two-dimensional surface to create and sustain a relationship between form and content, surface and subject matter.

One of the artists who was most likely introduced to Blakelock's work through the 1947 Whitney retrospective is Franz Kline, an artist whose work is as dark and fragile as Blakelock's. Although it would be another three years before he would have his aesthetic breakthrough, in which he unveiled a black and white gestural aesthetic, Kline was clearly struck by the bitumen-induced darkness of Blakelock's surfaces. As Glyn Vincent puts it, "Pollock's favorite American artist was Ryder and one of Kline's was none other than Blakelock."[13] So affected was Kline by Blakelock that he urged his Long Island collector, David Orr, to acquire Blakelock's work for his collection.[14]

It is perhaps not surprising that Kline would have been attracted to Blakelock. Although Kline is acknowledged as one of the great abstract expressionists, his work is, in comparison to that of Pollock, de Kooning, Rothko, Barnett Newman, Still, and Motherwell, underappreciated by curators, art historians, and art critics. While his contemporaries enjoy a veritable publishing cottage industry, books and exhibition catalogues on Kline are few and far between.[15] Like Blakelock, Kline suffers from the misperception that his work is limited; that he is a one-trick pony who happened upon a style in 1950 and continued to work and rework that style until his sudden and premature death in 1961, at only fifty-one. And like Blakelock's, Kline's legacy seems to have become less and less relevant to artistic practice as the years go by.

But perhaps the most important similarity between Blakelock and Kline is that they do not fit comfortably within the historical categories they currently occupy.[16] Blakelock is assumed by many art historians to be a lover of nature in the conventional nineteenth-century manner, but an artist possessed with an inner vision that anticipates twentieth-century modernist movements. Similarly, Kline is regarded as an orthodox gesture painter, expressing himself in calligraphic writings writ large on canvases with naturalistic associations. Kline's artistic practice, however, is nothing if not the initial tremors of the failure of modernism.[17] And so for all of Blakelock's aesthetic progressive prescience and Kline's self-confident abstract canvases, neither is best understood within the modernist paradigm of formal reduction and purity, with its obsession with optical experience and anticorporality. This modernist reductionism threatened to become iconoclastic in its rejection of the physicality of painting as an

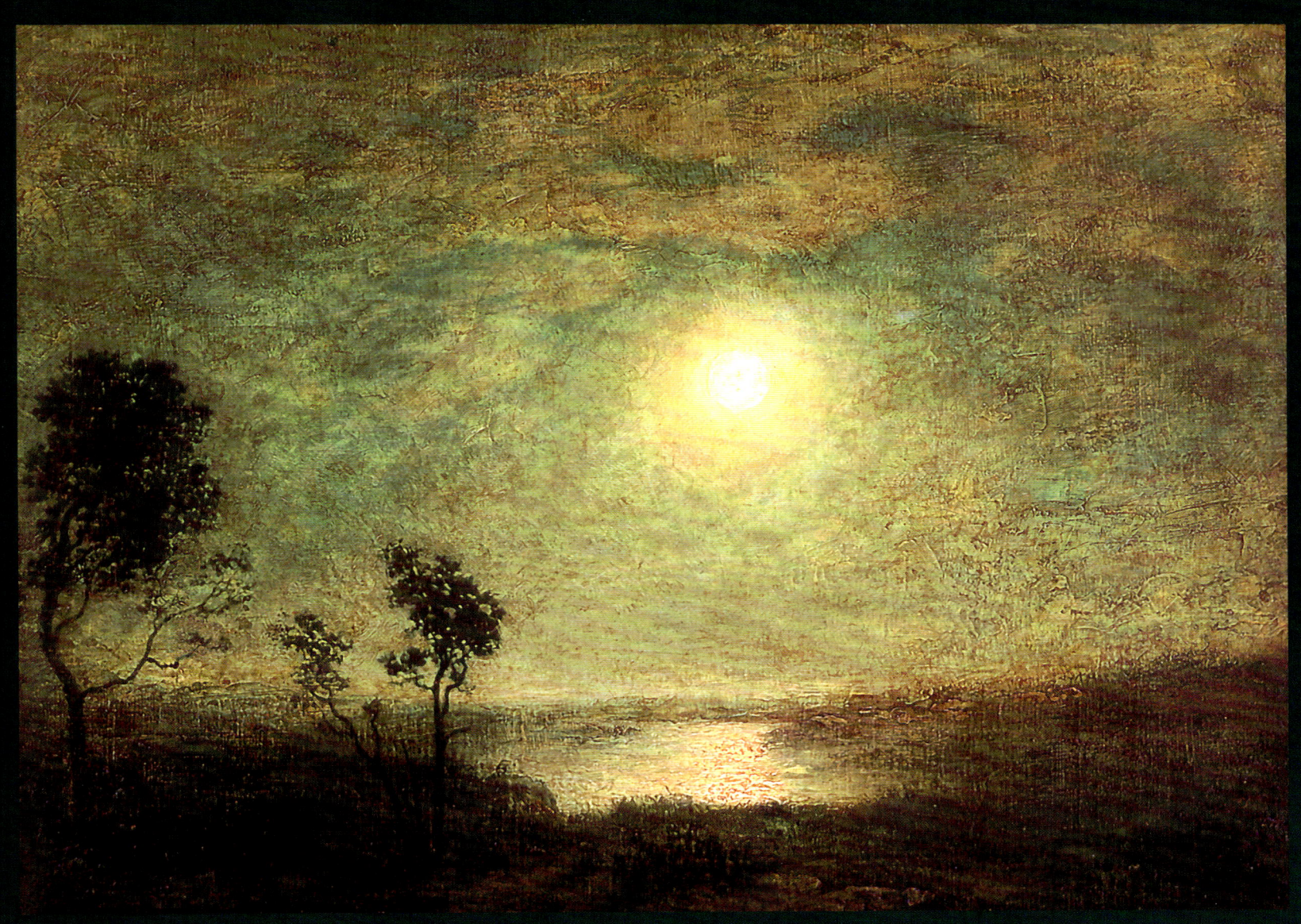

17 *Moonlight, 1886–1895*

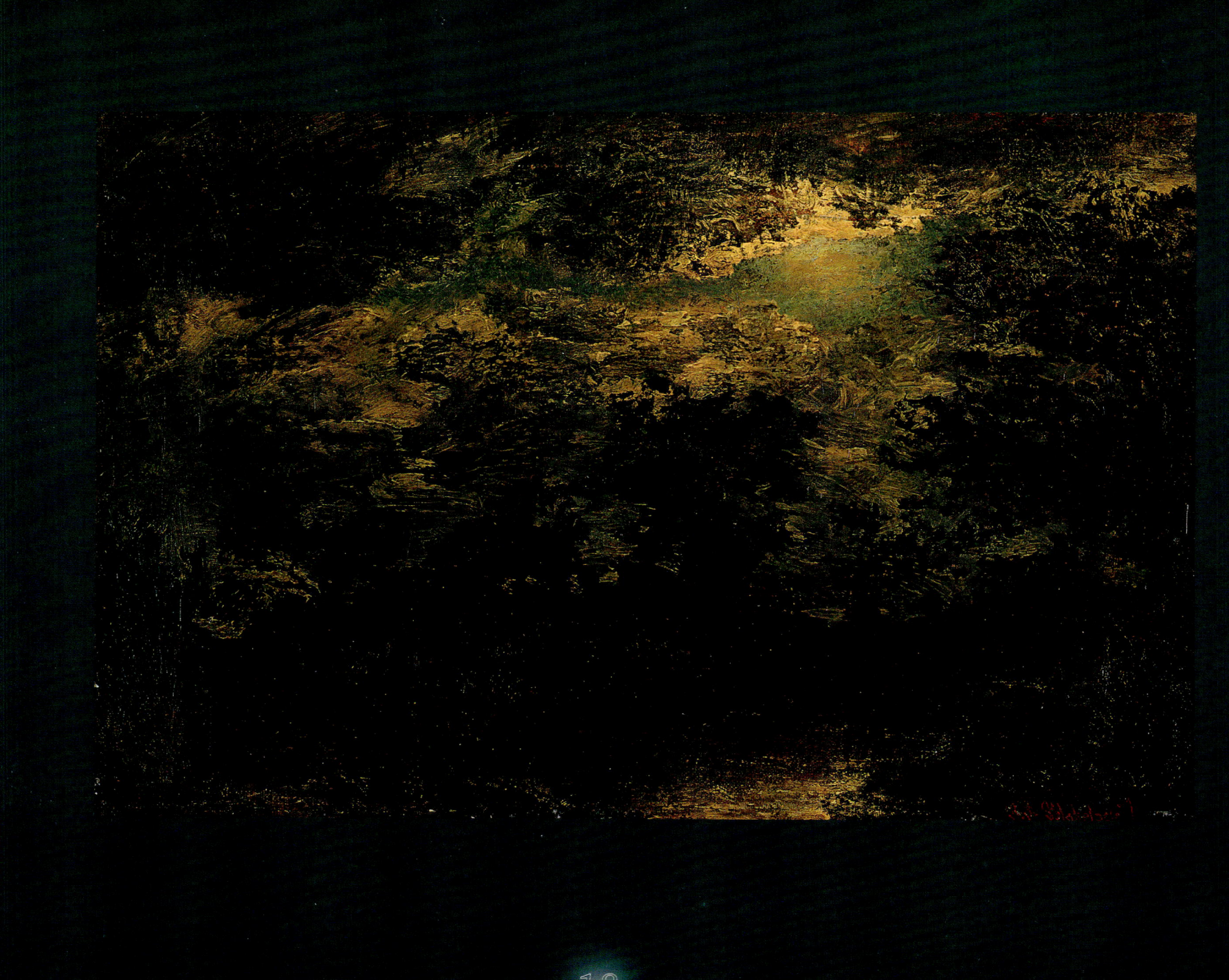

18 *Moonlight, Silver and Old Lace,* about 1880s

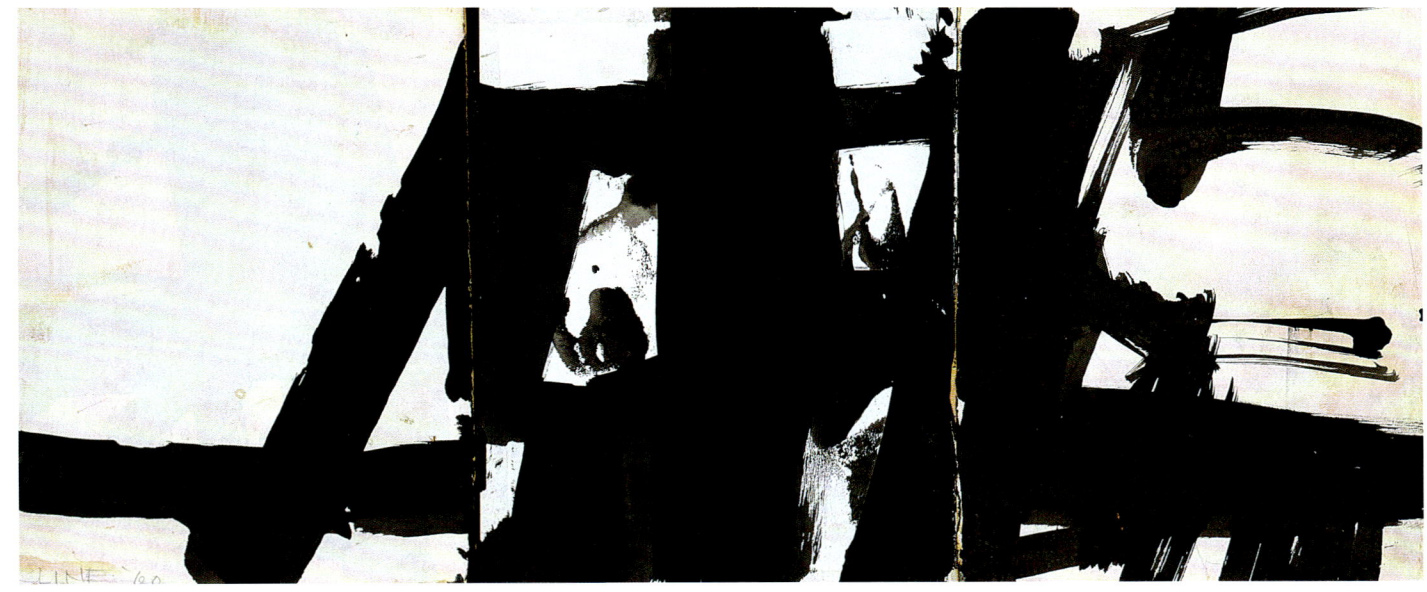

artifact and in its utopian desire for direct experience and pure transcendence.[18]

Both Kline's and Blakelock's paintings are often read in ways that obscure their aesthetic presence. Looking at Kline's paintings might be helpful in sorting out how to experience Blakelock's. First, Kline's paintings cannot be explained as abstractions of Kline's observations of the landscape, as they are often interpreted. The titles of his paintings, such as *Study for Shenandoah Wall* and *New York, N.Y.* (figs. 8 and 9), seem to be attractive hooks on which critics hang their interpretations of Kline's black and white compositions as opaque and disguised landscapes. This interpretation is also predicated on the mistaken view that Kline's paintings are calligraphic; that is, that they are black characters painted on a white ground. This

Fig. 8. FRANZ KLINE, *Study for Shenandoah Wall*, 1960, ink on three sheets of paper mounted on cardboard, 10½ × 25 in., Sheldon Memorial Art Gallery and Sculpture Garden, University of Nebraska–Lincoln, UNL—Olga N. Sheldon Acquisition Trust, 1984, U-3575.

mistake is easily made in viewing Kline's work in reproduction. A close examination of these paintings, however, reveals that neither black nor white can be easily or consistently established as foreground or background. Both white and black take turns exerting precedence, which gives the canvases an undulating tension, a quality that Kline used to refer to as "locking in the corners." This tension is located at the margins, giving the sense that just below the surface, in places such as where the black and white brushstrokes meet, the painting will burst

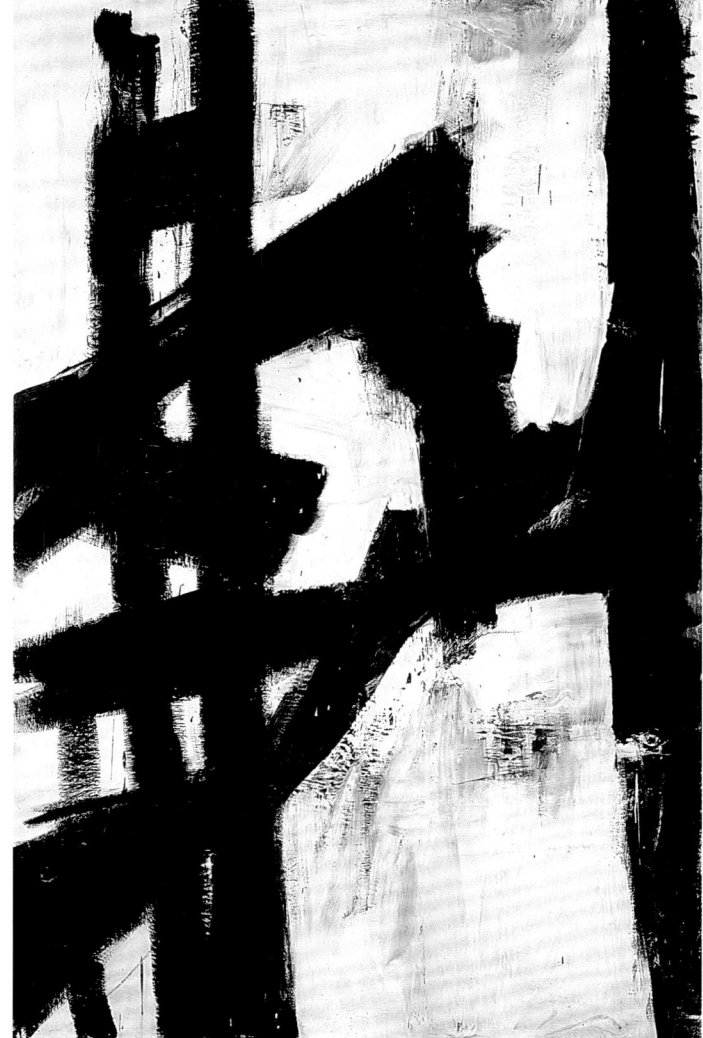

Fig. 9. FRANZ KLINE, *New York, N.Y.*, 1953, oil on canvas, 79 × 50½ in., Albright-Knox Art Gallery, Buffalo, New York, Gift of Seymour H. Knox Jr., 1956.

apart under pressure. The overall image of the painting is the result of these bulging edges.

Blakelock's paintings require the same kind of disciplined viewing. Their complexity is obscured if they are regarded too easily as simply part of the nineteenth-century fascination with Nature. Geske argues, rightly I believe, that

> Eventually Blakelock's vision becomes an exclusively internal experience. In his landscapes the skies, trees and waters become abstractions of these natural elements. Color, drawing and texture, light and space become self sufficient elements in his work.[19]

To view these paintings as landscapes, as the sum total of traditional elements of land, sea, sky, trees, light source, and so on, is to somehow give the image too much emphasis—an emphasis that made his moonlight paintings seemingly so easy to copy, imitate, and forge. As Geske says about the classic moonlight paintings:

> In undertaking a discussion of Blakelock's moonlight subjects, it is necessary to look at them with more care than has been customary, for they are richer and more various than the stereotype would indicate. Their impact and quality is based on Blakelock's acute receptivity to the phenomena of night. There is no sense of place in them, except the subjective "place" of the painter's imagination. Romantic in the fullest sense of the word, they are still free of the traditional apparatus of natural drama or literary allusion.[20]

This is not unlike the problems that Kline's work has encountered. It too has experienced its share of forgeries,

forgeries that are predicated on a stereotyped misunderstanding of Kline's work; namely, that it is images. Blakelock's paintings, like Kline's, are built in a certain way that their forgers and copyists seem to know little about.

Each painting begins as a potential failure for Kline. An initial mark becomes a problematic start, which becomes a challenge for him to overcome to create and sustain a formal balance. Each painting is an opportunity to win or achieve or, as Kline himself called it, "pull off" a new aesthetic balance.[21] So too with Blakelock. The landscapes, seascapes, moonlights, Indian encampments, and the like are the first strokes, or perhaps better put, they are the playing field on which Blakelock attempts to achieve as tense and tight a compositional balance as possible. Like Kline's, Blakelock's power lies in the edges, in the ways that the trees and the sky sit right next to each other, in the way that the sky pushes and pushes forward against the silhouettes of the trees. Perhaps this is what Kline saw when he looked at Blakelock's paintings. The limitations of Blakelock's and Kline's subject matter is not the result of a lack of imagination or of falling into a comfortable style. It results from their desire to achieve and re-achieve visual harmony again and again with each canvas, which makes the apparent repetitiveness and redundancy of the *whatness* of the painting (the subject and image) much less important than the *howness*. De Kooning once said that his ideal mode of painting would be to spend his entire life on a single canvas, painting and scraping off, painting and scraping off. This approach describes Blakelock and Kline as well.

IV

Painting has throughout the twentieth century attracted detractors, despite, or perhaps because of, its powerful presence. Beginning with Marcel Duchamp's famous declaration that painting was dead, many artists and critics have sought to transcend its materiality on one hand or to negate its immateriality on the other. Artists since the early 1950s have had an ambivalent relationship with painting. While it was serving as a heroic means of affirming individual identity for the abstract expressionists in the early 1950s, its sincerity and seriousness were also being undermined by such ironists as Jasper Johns and Robert Rauschenberg, both of whom were more interested in painting as a cultural construct than as a craft. This perspective has brought with it constant declarations by critics, scholars, and artists that painting is dead, that it has either reached the end of the modernist rope of formal innovation or become incapable of giving aesthetic form to contemporary experience. This view has been the implicit, and at times explicit, belief that emanates from postmodernism. It has held sway for the past thirty years, a belief in which "content" reigns; "craft" and "formal" considerations are too quickly dismissed as vestiges of a bankrupt modernism; and an ironic distance is taken toward the Good, the True, and the Beautiful. However, there has also been stiff resistance to this postmodern marginalization of painting. Reconsidering Blakelock's works in light of this emerging contemporary revitalization of painting, a trend in which artists have sought to reassert painting's distinctive expressive capacities without resuscitating modernism, might play an important role in this project.

Cuban-born, Los Angeles–based artist Enrique Martínez Celaya works in a variety of artistic media—printmaking, photography, sculpture, and painting[22]—but it is painting that is the center of his artistic practice. Martínez Celaya's painting is neither abstract nor figurative. In fact, it might be best to describe it as both, not simply as representational or exclusively figurative. Like Blakelock, painting for Martínez Celaya is an act of the imagination. And as with Kline, his work on the canvas begins on the canvas, not in preliminary sketches and plans. Martínez Celaya's painting, then, is the product of intuition, the result of a "skirmish" on the canvas, as critic Harold Rosenberg referred to the work of the abstract expressionists in his famous 1952 essay "The American Action Painters."[23]

I read Geske's 1974 essay on Blakelock while doing research at Martínez Celaya's studio last year, and it spurred many opportunities to talk with him about Blakelock and painting. Martínez Celaya has had a serious and abiding interest in Blakelock's work. It is thus not surprising that while we looked at his paintings in process in his studio that our discussion gravitated toward Geske's essay and Blakelock's distinctive pictorial space. Like Kline, whose exclusive use of black and white enamel paint after 1950 makes his work appear dark and brooding like Blakelock's, so too Martínez Celaya, especially the work that he produced between 2000 and 2003, called *The October Cycle*, which consists of twenty-three *black* paintings made of tar, feathers, and oil paint.[24] Like Kline's black enamel, Martínez Celaya's tar possesses a certain kinship with Blakelock's bitumen (fig. 10, *Bonn II*). But this relationship goes much deeper.

The paintings in Martínez Celaya's studio in front of which we discussed Blakelock's achievements were not black. They were gigantic canvases on which numerous oil and wax glazes had been applied to the surface to create a luminous bluish hue

Fig. 10. Enrique Martínez Celaya, *Bonn II*, 2001, oil, tar, and feathers on canvas, 67 × 72 in., Collection of Andrew Kassoy, New York.

with a glowing light. As in Blakelock's work, the basic vocabulary for Martínez Celaya's paintings is the landscape—forests, rivers, sun, and moonlight—and figures, usually a single adolescent male, often nude. These compositions have a curious unreality about them, or perhaps better put, a *suprareality*. Their end results as finished paintings rarely resemble how they were initially conceived. Figures emerge and disappear on the canvas, and so each final painting is not merely the end result of numerous versions but seems to hover tensely as an artifact in the process of becoming, perhaps interrupted, frozen, or suspended. As Willem de Kooning once observed, "Content is a glimpse of something, an encounter like a flash. It's very tiny—very tiny, content."[25]

The flash of content in Martínez Celaya's canvases seems mystical. This mystical suprareality is also characteristic of Blakelock's work. In fact, Geske observes

> Blakelock cared comparatively little for form, either in his composition or in his rendering of particular objects. He was absorbed in other things. And this is something that many people will like to appreciate. There is something in nature besides form, something that in many minds is infinitely superior to form. Many think that if you paint a tree people ought to know what kind of tree it is, whether oak or hop hornbeam or mulberry. Blakelock has no such idea. . . . He saw other things in nature, and one good thing about an appreciation of him is that it shows that there are other things than form to see.[26]

Blakelock by no means denied the world of appearances, as did many of his utopian, modernist successors. But appearances are not all the world is made up of, and Blakelock's form implies this. Transcendence is sought, not by denying this world of appearances, but in delving into appearance, looking into it, *through* it, using it as a real metaphor, or a "real allegory," as Gustave Courbet entitled his masterpiece of 1855. Geske suggests, "there is no sense of 'plein air' in Blakelock's world. It is almost completely subjective in concept and exists only as the construct of a highly poetic imagination."[27] Geske continues, "it can be said that the examination of hundreds of Blakelock's

skies, trees and figures in their minutest detail, has established that they are not so much the representations of these things as they are conjurations, dictated by a highly sensory appreciation of their visual character."[28] And this approach to transcendence is one in which Martínez Celaya's work also participates. His images are indeed conjurations, not representations. Like Blakelock, who used the traditional and conventional nineteenth-century tropes of the natural landscape to explore a reality beyond, Martínez Celaya uses the romantic images and symbols of birchwood trees, forests, rivers, dusk, and sunrise, and he uses them to explore a reality beyond appearances, a truth, or *Geist*, as Hegel called it.

An important topic of my conversations with Martínez Celaya about Blakelock had to do with the complexity of Blakelock's pictorial space, a pictorial space with which all painters struggle. For Martínez Celaya, the curious suprareality that does not deny the world of appearances, but uses it symbolically and analogically, is wrought through his distinctive development of pictorial space that embodies or points to a deeper reality. The conventional Renaissance-style pictorial structure, in which the surface becomes a picture window through which figures, whether human beings or trees or what have you, interact in a consistent space does not exist for Martínez Celaya. Such space is naturalizing, demystifying, rationalized. And such naturalized space is the basis for the modernist rejection of the empirical world in favor of a transcendent realm of "pure form," "pure spirit."[29] In contrast, neither Blakelock's nor Martínez Celaya's canvases reject the world of appearances, although they are not defined by it—either by accepting or rejecting it. An in-depth examination of Martínez Celaya's paintings reveals a dynamic pictorial surface,

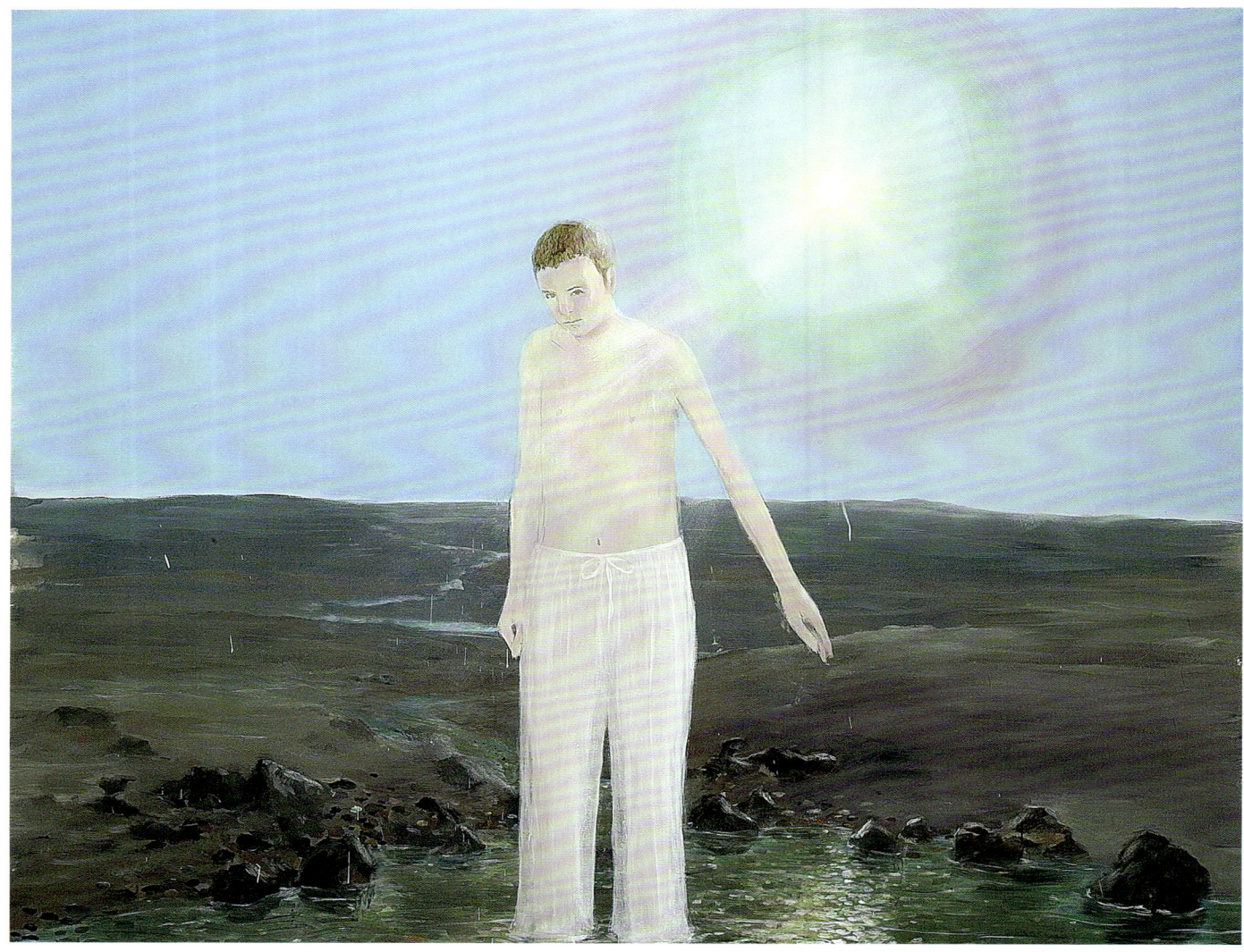

Fig. 11. Enrique Martínez Celaya, *The long-for sun*, 2007, oil and wax on canvas,
78 × 100 in., Courtesy of Liverpool Street Gallery, East Sydney, Australia.

particularly exemplified in the relationship of the foreground, middleground, and background that reveals a space that does not so much recede from foreground to background as turn back toward the foreground in an oval space; from the bottom of the canvas to the top, space is shallow, then deeper, and then returns to shallow. This oval shaped spatial projection gives the pictorial surface a subtle yet distinctive and unavoidable tension. For example, in *The long-for sun* (2007) (fig. 11), the mysterious figure is not placed in a landscape; it is woven into the fabric of the surface, such that removing it would not merely leave an empty landscape, but would destroy the entire surface of the painting. The figure, like many of those in Martínez Celaya's paintings, complicates a reading of the image as operating comfortably in Renaissance space, particularly at the edges of the figure, where sky and landscape bleed onto it, flattening out the composition and making it more difficult to read the pictures as merely a narrative, a story in which the figure is playing a role. Rather, the figure and all the other elements in the painting (trees, rivers, ponds, sun, rainbow, etc.) do not illustrate Truth or Reality; they embody it, project it, reveal it, uncover or unconceal it, as Heidegger would say, since "Art then is the becoming and happening of truth."[30]

Blakelock's paintings benefit from a similar scrutiny. Blakelock's figures are not placed in an environment any more than his trees are a naturalistic backdrop for some kind of conventional pictorial narrative. His landscapes are neither optimistic idealizations of a passive nature that are available for human use nor representations of Nature as the sublime or divine. Because his rejection of nature, a key aspect of modernism, is always incomplete and ambivalent, Blakelock remains too traditional for modernist art historians. However, he was and

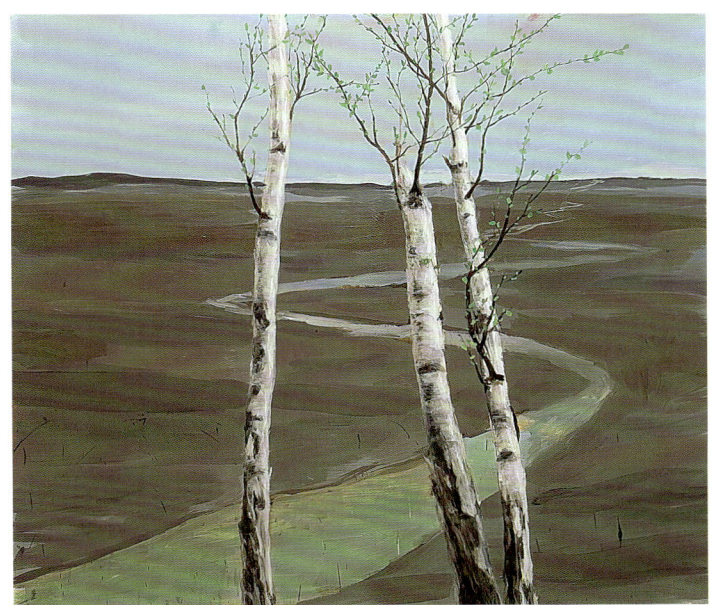

Fig. 12. Enrique Martínez Celaya, *The Valley*, 2007, oil and wax on canvas, 66 × 72 in., Courtesy of Sara Meltzer Gallery, New York.

remains too visionary to conform to typical nineteenth-century responses to the landscape. The landscape is simultaneously more and less than imagined and invented; it is metaphorical, analogical, or conjectured. This is the same experience I have in front of Martínez Celaya's *The Valley* (2007) (fig. 12), in which three birch trees at first glance seem to occupy the foreground of the large, square-shaped painting. But on closer attention the three trees sit on the surface, stretching from the bottom to the top of the canvas. The trees, then, become objects of contemplation, imbued with symbolic presence. The work is an icon of some

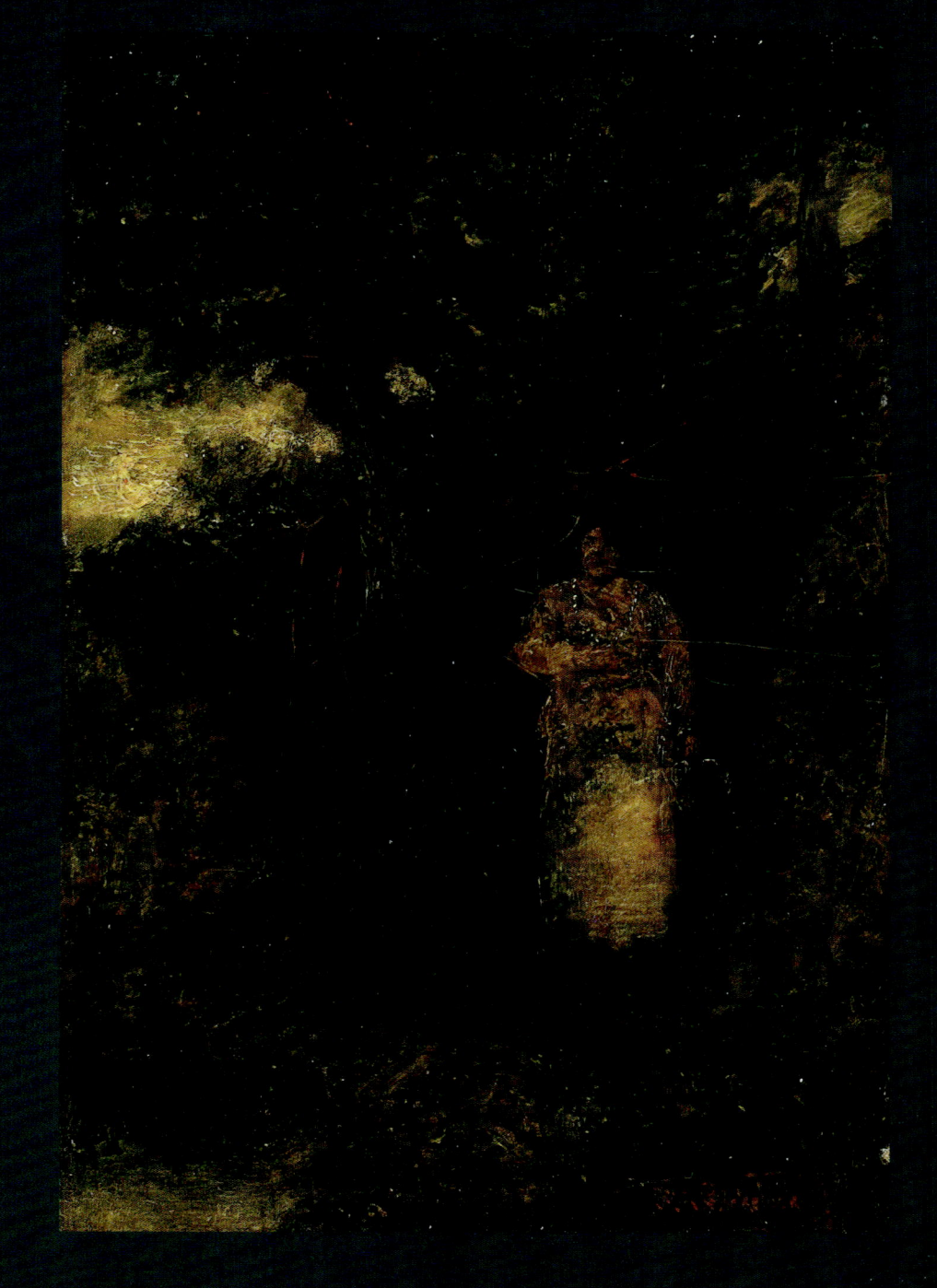

19 *Going to the Spring*, undated

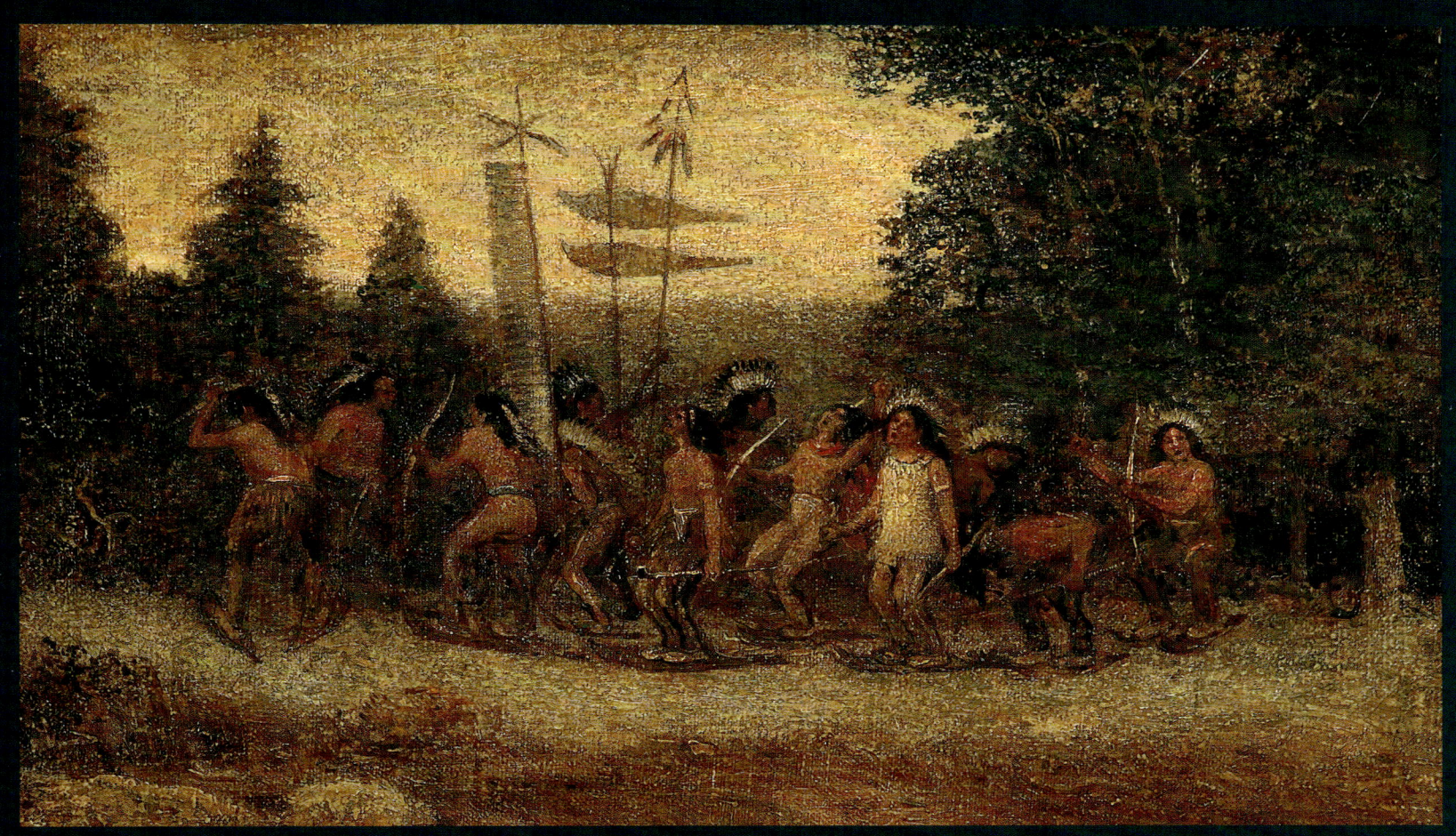

20 *The Snowshoe Dance, 1879*

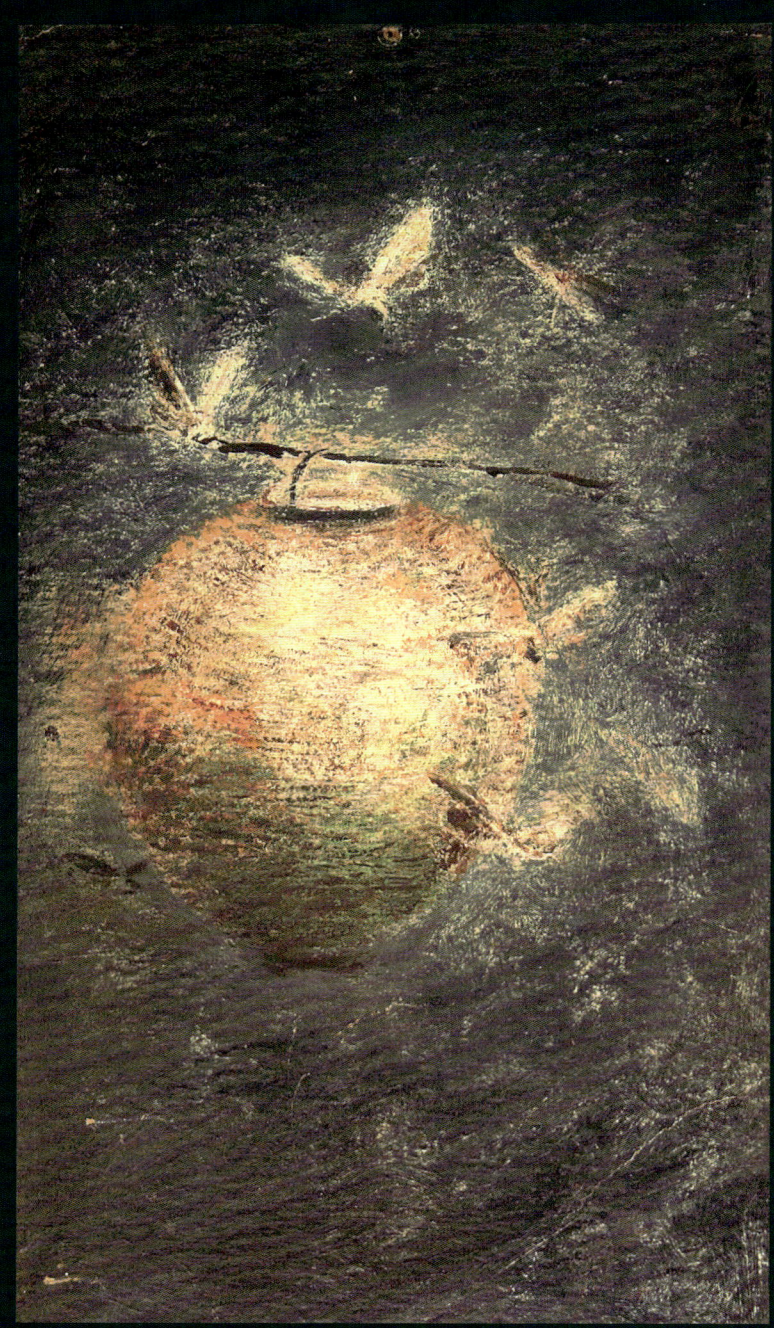

21 *Japanese Lantern and Moths,* undated

kind, a devotional painting in which the three trees relate to the valley in a symbolical, not merely natural, way.

And then there is Martínez Celaya's light—a soft, enveloping, glowing light that has characterized the work he has produced during the period he has worked in Florida. This light, as evidenced in such paintings as *The long-for sun,* is similar to that of Blakelock's, here described by Geske: "It is perfectly clear that this is not the light of the Luminist painters. It is not a light that clarifies and defines."[31] It is not the light of rationalism, of demystification, of empiricism. It is the light of revelation, conversion. It is not the light of the Renaissance; it is the light of the Russian icon. It is the light of belief, of faith, revealed or unveiled through the means of a different kind of clarity, a different kind of reason. This is, I argue, as true for Blakelock as it is for Martínez Celaya.

v

Blakelock's hold on reality was as tenuous as his paintings' hold on their subjects. His compositions are poetic forays into the transcendent unknown through the natural world. It is possible that it is Blakelock, rather than Ryder, who has the potential for influencing twenty-first-century painting. The present situation is a global, market-obsessed, postmodernist, spiritualized, mystical, and fetishized pluralist culture in which such modernist worldviews as Ryder's, with his confidence in literary, religious, and romantic iconography, might not have the same kind of impact on contemporary painters as the tentative, ambivalent complexities of Blakelock's slightly—but never completely—unhinged forays into the world of appearances, mysticism, and imagination. David Bjelajac observes, "in Blakelock's paintings, the quiet presence of Native Americans,

whom he clearly admired, merges with a religious, cosmic feeling of spiritual transcendence, symbolized by the pale glowing light of the moon."[32] This kind of mysticism, derived from a pantheistic, Swedenborgian Christianity that also influenced George Inness, bears more resemblance to contemporary spirituality than the "art as religion" and "religion as art" metaphors of modernism, of which Ryder was not only more conversant than Blakelock, but whose work assimilated them more easily. Ryder remains a protomodernist in a way that Blakelock never was. Blakelock's lack of formal study, disinterest in Europe, and wounded, humbled life, might be advantageous for postmodern painters eager to continue to explore formal complexities and challenges of the craft of painting without the residue of an all too confident modernist mythologizing.

Perhaps the integrity of painting as a contemporary postmodern practice can be found in learning the aesthetic lessons of a self-taught artist who left virtually no artistic philosophy and had no students, who lost a fight with schizophrenia, who loved music, who had a pantheistic love of the world and fascination with light, and who invested his paintings with a mysticism that jarred both the rationalistic scientism and historicism and the irrationalist Neoplatonism of late nineteenth-century culture. Contemporary painting needs a little more faith and belief, a little more doubt and risk. Painting is ultimately a religious practice. Simply to put oil paint on canvas calls forth a Kierkegaardian risk of faith that the result will add up to more than the sum of the banal materials that produced it. I am convinced that this is what Franz Kline, Enrique Martínez Celaya, and many other painters have seen when they have looked at a painting by R. A. Blakelock. And it is what needs to be seen by the current generation.

Daniel A. Siedell is assistant professor of modern and contemporary art history, theory, and criticism at the University of Nebraska–Omaha.

NOTES

1. Quoted in Thomas B. Hess, *Willem de Kooning* (New York: Museum of Modern Art, 1968), 145–46.

2. Wayne Craven, *American Art: History and Culture* (New York: Abrams, 1994), 362.

3. Glyn Vincent, *The Unknown Night: The Genius and Madness of R. A. Blakelock, An American Painter* (New York: Grove Press, 2003), 304.

4. Lloyd Goodrich, *Ralph Albert Blakelock* (New York: Whitney Museum of American Art, 1947), 17.

5. Ibid.

6. Ibid.

7. Robert Coates, "Blakelock," *The New Yorker,* May 3, 1947, 73.

8. William Seitz, *Abstract Expressionist Painting in America* (1955; Cambridge, MA: Harvard University Press, 1983).

9. Seitz, 154.

10. Ibid.

11. Norman A. Geske, "The Development of the Painter's Style," in *Ralph Albert Blakelock, 1847–1919* (Lincoln, NE: Sheldon Memorial Art Gallery, 1974), 18.

12. Arthur Danto, "Midas Touched," *Bookforum* (Spring 2003), 8.

13. Vincent, 305. See also Harry F. Gaugh, *Franz Kline* (New York: Abbeville Press, 1985), 129.

14. Abraham A. Davidson, *Ralph Albert Blakelock* (University Park, PA: The Pennsylvania State University Press, 1996), 204.

15. Harry F. Gaugh, *Franz Kline: The Vital Gesture* (Cincinnati Art Museum; New York: Abbeville Press, 1985); David Anfam, *Franz Kline: 1950–1961* (Houston: The Menil Collection, 1996); Stephen C. Foster, *Franz Kline: Art and the Structure of Identity* (Tapies Foundation; Electa: 1994); *Franz Kline, 1910–1962* (Skira, 2003).

16. See Daniel A. Siedell, "Kline contra Kline," *Art Criticism* 12, no. 1 (1996): 83–94. See also Daniel A. Siedell, "An Excavation of Tenth Street: The Historiography of the New York School and the Failure of Modernism" (PhD diss., The University of Iowa, 1995).

17. This is the argument of Stephen C. Foster in *Franz Kline: Art and the Structure of Identity*.

18. Peter Weibel, "An End to the 'End of Art'?: On the Iconoclasm of Modern Art," in *Iconoclash: Beyond the Image Wars in Science, Religion and Art,* ed. Bruno Latour and Peter Weibel (Cambridge, MA: MIT Press, 2002).

19. Norman A. Geske, *Beyond Madness: The Art of Ralph Blakelock, 1847–1919* (Lincoln and London: University of Nebraska Press, 2007), 69.

20. Ibid., 77.

21. Foster, *Franz Kline: Art and the Structure of Identity,* 15–39.

22. Daniel A. Siedell, *Enrique Martínez Celaya: Early Work* (Delray Beach, FL: Whale and Star, 2006).

23. Harold Rosenberg, "The American Action Painters" (1952) in *The Tradition of the New* (New York, 1959).

24. Daniel A. Siedell, *Enrique Martínez Celaya: The October Cycle, 2000–2003* (Lincoln, NE: Sheldon Memorial Art Gallery; Marquand Books, 2003).

25. "Content Is a Glimpse," in Hess, *Willem de Kooning,* 151.

26. Quoted in Norman A. Geske, *Beyond Madness.*

27. Geske, "The Development of the Painter's Style," 30.

28. Ibid., 25.

29. Kirk Varnedoe, *Pictures of Nothing: Abstract Art Since Pollock* (National Gallery of Art; Princeton, NJ: Princeton University Press, 2006), 99.

30. Martin Heidegger, "The Origin of the Work of Art," in *Poetry, Language, Thought,* trans. Albert Hofstadter (New York: Harper and Row, 1971), 71.

31. Ibid., 30.

32. David Bjelajac, *American Art: A Cultural History* (Upper Saddle River, NJ: Prentice Hall, 2005), 280.

1847 October 15. Ralph Albert Blakelock born to Caroline Oliveria Carey, about whom very little is known, and Ralph B. Blakelock, who at that time was a carpenter (later a policeman), and who in 1861 became a homeopathic physician at Christopher Street, New York City. The first "Albert" among twelve in the Blakelock family to have the first name Ralph. (Vincent, 36.)

1864 Enters Free Academy of the City of New York. (Now the City College of New York.)

1866–72 Period of his initial style, that of the Hudson River School.

1867 Exhibits for the first time at the National Academy of Design, where he shows at least once a year until 1873.

1868 Earliest dated work, *Sunrise* (North Carolina State Museum).

1869 Journeys to the American West, where he becomes enchanted with the American Indian and the theme of the primeval forest.

1872 Possibly a second trip to the West (no definite record).

1873–78 *City Scene* introduces the second period of Blakelock's career; signatures are scratched into the surface of the paint.

1877 Marries Cora Rebecca Bailey, whom he had known as a child during Vermont summers. Moves to East Orange, New Jersey, to "draw the countryside." First child, Carl, born.

1879–83 Transitional phase; artist changes his signature, which becomes bolder, orange-red, and surrounded by an arrowhead or fish.

1883–98 Mature period.

1890 Suffers first mental breakdown, and on March 25 is taken by ambulance to the Long Island Hospital, Brooklyn.

1899 Last of nine children born to the couple dies. On September 12, Blakelock is admitted to Long Island Hospital, suffering from dementia praecox.

1901 June, transferred to Middletown State Hospital for the Insane in Middletown, New York. Exhibits at Lotus Club, New York. Second exhibition at Lotus Club, New York.

1911 Transferred to Dr. Packer's Sanitarium, Riverdale, New York.

1913 Chicago, Moulton and Ricketts Gallery, group exhibition with George Inness and Alexander H. Wyant. Elected an associate member, National Academy of Design.

1916 New York, Reinhardt Gallery exhibition, where Blakelock visits the show. Elected to a full Academician by the National Academy of Design. Subsequently lives in a private sanitarium in Englewood, New Jersey.

1918 Returns to Middletown, where most of his remaining life is spent in confinement.

1919 August 19, dies in a cottage in the Adirondacks at age 72, the "most celebrated artist in America."

SELECTED BIBLIOGRAPHY

For the comprehensive biography and bibliography, please consult the following:

Norman A. Geske, *Beyond Madness: The Art of Ralph Blakelock, 1847–1919*. Lincoln, NE, and London: University of Nebraska Press, 2007. 336 pages.

Additional bibliographic information can be found in:

Abraham A. Davidson, *Ralph Albert Blakelock*. University Park, PA: The Pennsylvania State University Press, 1996, 235–240.

Glyn Vincent, *The Unknown Night: The Genius and Madness of R. A. Blakelock, An American Painter*. New York: Grove Press, 2003, 339–342.

CHECKLIST

*Sheldon venue only
**National Academy of Design venue only

59th Street in 1864
Undated
Oil on panel
7 × 11⅜ in.
Des Moines Art Center Permanent Collection, Gift of Carl Weeks, 1962.19 (NBI-39.I)

A Mountain Stream
1872–80
Oil on canvas
10 × 12 in.
Joslyn Art Museum, Omaha, Nebraska, Gift of Mrs. Harold Gifford, 1961.241 (NBI-53.II)

At Nature's Mirror
About 1880
Oil on canvas
16⅛ × 24 in.
Smithsonian American Art Museum, Gift of William T. Evans, 1909.7.5 (NBI-242.I)

Bee and Thistle
Undated
Oil on canvas
19 × 15 in.
Private collection, Connecticut

**Brook by Moonlight*
Before 1891
Oil on canvas
72⅛ × 48⅛ in.
Lent by the Toledo Museum of Art, Gift of Mr. and Mrs. Edward Drummond Libbey, 1916.4 (NBI-703.I)

Early Autumn
Undated
Oil on canvas
29 × 38 in.
Muskegon Museum of Art, Hackley Picture Fund Purchase, 1912.5 (NBI-978.II)

Forest Fire
Undated
Oil on canvas
22 × 36 in.
Lent by Richard T. Sharp

Going to the Spring
Undated
Oil on canvas
8 × 5¾ in.
The JPMorgan Chase Art Collection, 36595 (NBI-1030.II)

Harvest Moon
About 1890
Oil on canvas
16 × 23 in.
Gift of Lauren Chase Eastman, Collection of the Lauren Rogers Museum of Art, Laurel, Mississippi, 27.18 (NBI-184.II)

Heavy Woods—Moonlight
Undated
Oil on board
6⅛ × 9¾ in.
Sheldon Memorial Art Gallery and Sculpture Garden, University of Nebraska–Lincoln, UNL—Gift of Mrs. Olga N. Sheldon, 1973, U-3286 (NBI-157.I)

Indian Camp
Undated
Oil on canvas
16⅝ × 36⅝ in.
Collection of Mary Ann Apicella and Jack Hollihan (NBI-204.II)

Indian Encampment
Undated
Oil on canvas
9½ × 13½ in.
Gift of Mr. C. R. Smith, 1967.030, Permanent collection, Snite Museum of Art, University of Notre Dame (NBI-2.II)

Japanese Lantern and Moths
Undated
Oil on board
8 × 4⅝ in.
Collection of Mr. and Mrs. Walter Blakelock Wilson (NBI-1851.I)

Landscape
Undated
Oil on canvas
16 × 24 in.
The Detroit Institute of Arts, Bequest of Dexter M. Ferry Jr., 60.67 (NBI-222.I)

Maiden in the Mist
Undated
Oil on board
7⅛ × 21⅞ in.
The Grey Collection, Brookville, New York (NBI-2021.II)

Moonlight
1886–1895
Oil on canvas
28⅛ × 37⅛ in.
The Corcoran Gallery of Art, Washington, DC,
William A. Clark Collection, 26.8 (NBI-21.I)

Moonlight
About 1880s
Oil on canvas
22 × 27 in.
Sheldon Memorial Art Gallery and Sculpture
Garden, University of Nebraska–Lincoln, NAA—
Nelle Cochrane Woods Memorial, 1960, N-127
(NBI-304.II)

Moonlight
1885–1889
Oil on canvas
27⅛ × 32 in.
Brooklyn Museum, Dick S. Ramsay Fund, 42.171
(NBI-356.I)

Moonlight Landscape
Late 1880s–early 1890s
Oil on wood panel
5⅞ × 9½ in.
The Phillips Collection, Washington, DC, 0143
(NBI-245.II)

Moonlight, Silver and Old Lace
Undated (about 1880s)
Oil on canvas
16⅛ × 24⅛ in.
Santa Barbara Museum of Art, Gift of Mr. and
Mrs. John D. Graham, 1947.22.1 (NBI-95.II)

**Moonlight Sonata*
About 1889–92
Oil on canvas
30⅜ × 22 in.
Museum of Fine Arts, Boston. The Hayden
Collection—Charles Henry Hayden Fund

Pegasus
Before 1913
Oil on board
9 × 13 in.
Denver Art Museum, The Edward and Tullah
Hanley Memorial, Gift to the People of Denver
and the Area 1974.420 (NBI-68.I)

**Rockaway Beach, Long Island, New York*
About 1870
Oil on panel
12 × 20 in.
Museum of Fine Arts, Boston. Gift of Maxim
Karolik for the M. and M. Karolik Collection of
American Paintings, 1815–1865

Rocky Mountains
About 1871
Oil on canvas
33 × 55 in.
Courtesy of Berkshire Museum, Pittsfield,
Massachusetts (NBI-198.I)

Seal Rocks
Undated
Oil on canvas mounted to hardboard
42¼ × 30¼ in.
Collection of the Paine Art Center and Gardens,
Oshkosh, Wisconsin (NBI-595.II)

Shanties, Seventh Avenue at 55th St.
Undated
Oil on canvas
16¼ × 24¼ in.
Collection of Al and Lisa Schmitt, Los Angeles,
California (NBI-463.II)

St. Gabriel's Grotto, Isle of Jamaica
About 1872
Oil on canvas
36 × 24 in.
The James M. Cowan Collection of American Art,
The Parthenon Museum, Nashville, Tennessee,
29.2.15 (NBI-373.II)

Summer
Undated
Oil on board
4 × 12 in.
Collection of Jane and Carl H. Rohman, Lincoln,
Nebraska (NBI-167.I)

Sunset
1879–1883
Oil on canvas
27¼ × 37 in.
Memphis Brooks Museum of Art, Memphis,
Tennessee, Gift of Mr. and Mrs. Morrie A. Moss,
58.9 (NBI-72.I)

Sunset, Navarro Ridge, California Coast
1870–1879
Oil on canvas
36⅜ × 56⅜ in.
Smithsonian American Art Museum, Gift of
William T. Evans (NBI-243.I)

The Grotto
1880
Oil on canvas
36¼ × 56¼ in.
Chrysler Museum of Art, Norfolk, Virginia, Gift of
Walter P. Chrysler Jr., 71.620 (NBI-507.I)

**The Sun, Serene, Sinks into the Slumbrous Sea*
Undated
Oil on canvas
16 × 24 in.
Horace P. Wright Collection, Museum of Fine Arts,
Springfield, Massachusetts, W13.3 (NBI-224.I)

**The Vision of Life (Ghost Dance)*
1895–1897
Oil on canvas
21⅛ × 39⅜ in.
The Art Institute of Chicago, Charles H. and Mary F. S. Worcester Collection, 1947.55 (NBI-240.II)

Twilight
1898
Oil on canvas
20 × 30 in.
Collection of the Butler Institute of American Art, Youngstown, Ohio, Gift of H. H. Stambaugh, 1919, 919-0-103 (NBI-161.II)

Untitled (landscape)
Undated
Oil on board
6 × 8⅛ in.
Sheldon Memorial Art Gallery and Sculpture Garden, University of Nebraska–Lincoln, UNL—Gift of Mr. and Mrs. Davis R. Robinson in memory of John Frederick Degener, III, and Cynthia Davis Robinson Degener, U-2322 (NBI-955.I)

Untitled (landscape)
Undated
Oil on wood panel
5⅜ × 9¼ in.
Sheldon Memorial Art Gallery and Sculpture Garden, University of Nebraska–Lincoln, UNL—Gift of Mr. and Mrs. Davis R. Robinson in memory of John Frederick Degener, III, and Cynthia Davis Robinson Degener, U-2323 (NBI-956.I)

Untitled (landscape)
Undated
Oil on wood panel
5½ × 9⅜ in.
Sheldon Memorial Art Gallery and Sculpture Garden, University of Nebraska–Lincoln, UNL—Gift of Mr. and Mrs. Davis R. Robinson in memory of John Frederick Degener, III, and Cynthia Davis Robinson Degener, U-2326 (NBI-959.I)

Untitled (landscape)
About 1916
Oil on board
3⅞ × 5⅞ in.
Sheldon Memorial Art Gallery and Sculpture Garden, University of Nebraska–Lincoln, NAA—Nelle Cochrane Woods Memorial, Gift of Mr. and Mrs. Thomas C. Woods Jr., N-207 (NBI-305.I)

Untitled (landscape)
About 1918
Oil on cardboard
3¼ × 5½ in.
Sheldon Memorial Art Gallery and Sculpture Garden, University of Nebraska–Lincoln, NAA—Nelle Cochrane Woods Memorial, Gift of Mr. and Mrs. Thomas C. Woods Jr., N-208 (NBI-322.I)

Untitled (landscape)
About 1916
Oil on board
6 × 8⅛ in.
Sheldon Memorial Art Gallery and Sculpture Garden, University of Nebraska–Lincoln, NAA—Nelle Cochrane Woods Memorial, Gift of Mr. and Mrs. Thomas C. Woods Jr., N-212 (NBI-326.I)

Untitled (sunset landscape)
About 1917
Oil on board
8 × 8 in.
Sheldon Memorial Art Gallery and Sculpture Garden, University of Nebraska–Lincoln, NAA—Nelle Cochrane Woods Memorial, Gift of Mr. and Mrs. Thomas C. Woods Jr., N-213 (NBI-327.I)

Untitled (landscape)
Undated
Oil on panel
3⅝ × 5⅛ in.
Sheldon Memorial Art Gallery and Sculpture Garden, University of Nebraska–Lincoln, NAA—Gift of Mr. and Mrs. Carl H. Rohman, N-308 (NBI 413.I)

Violets
Undated
Oil on canvas
10 × 8 in.
Private collection (NBI-126.I)

Western Landscape
About 1871
Oil on canvas
34¼ × 60 in.
Collection of the Newark Museum, Gift of the Board of Directors, National Newark and Essex Bank, 1965, 65.34 (NBI-202.II)

Woodland Brook
1880s–1890s
Oil on canvas
16 × 24 in.
Collection Albright-Knox Art Gallery, Buffalo, New York, Gift of Elizabeth Elser Doolittle Charitable Trust, 1977, 1977:6 (NBI-434.I)